An Ordinary Town: *Extraordinary Neighbors*

Jill Osborn

Copyright © 2013 Jill Osborn

ISBN:0615922651
ISBN-13:9780615922652

DEDICATION

To my neighbors, who make our town extraordinary.

To my family and littles, Jaxy and Olliana. I especially want to thank my husband, who encourages all my dreams. Also, to my mom, who is an amazing writer and made this book possible.

CONTENTS

ACKNOWLEDGMENTS

Foreword from the Mayor of Clemmons and my brother, Nick Nelson:

Jill is a treasure hunter. All of my life, I have watched my sister find something where most people saw nothing. Growing up, our mom taught us to find something everyone could enjoy, or else risk playing alone. While I preferred playing army or sports, Jill liked sports and dress-up. However, Jill excelled at taking the enjoyable aspects of any game and tying it to another that we could all share in. I think my favorite was dodgeball on the trampoline.

High school was the first time I remember my sister extracting the best from an individual's personality. She would come to me and say, "Nick, the funniest thing just happened. You have to meet this person... ." She didn't want to keep her new find to herself. She just had to share. I think one reason she has always made friends so easily is because she has this incredible ability to embolden trust, largely on a subconscious level. Maybe people realize she is genuinely interested in them. So when Jill announced to our family that she wanted to be a reporter, it seemed as natural as a river flowing towards the ocean. Unfortunately, the occupation required her to be far from home and away from the ones she loved, and the ones who loved her. After learning her trade, Jill brought her reporting experiences home with her.

Jill has been developing her skills as a storyteller and treasure hunter all her life, finding the gifts inside each person she meets. It has been no surprise, when she did come back home to settle down and raise a family, that she would continue to seek out and find new people to befriend. Jill then found a way to share these new friends with everyone in her column and now this book. Every time I read her stories, I know that she is giving each reader the opportunity to find the same gems inside our neighbors that she has found. I am thankful that she wants, so enthusiastically, to share them, just as she has done all of her life.

INTRODUCTION

Do you remember the day you realized you were not invincible? I do. It was the day I miscarried. We went to our eight-week ultrasound appointment and saw our baby was merely the size of a six-week-old. At that point, I learned two lessons. I am not in control and the career I had worked so hard for meant little to me without my loved ones nearby. I did not want to make it big as a news anchor anymore. I did not want to sit at the news desk with not a single hair out of place. I wanted to curl up in a ball and never leave my bed. I wanted one thing. I wanted our baby.

One year later, love came crashing into my heart like a big ocean wave when I first saw my son. The outpouring emotion I had for this little boy who depended on me for his survival was endless. What was even more shocking was what happened when I had my second-- my daughter. I was worried I would not love her as much. However, that little girl looked at me and her angelic expression reached into the depths of my soul. Both babies changed everything. I would forever live my life for them.

While I clearly adored my new role as a stay-at-home mother, I found myself gravitating back toward the television as news stories flashed on the black box. I began thinking about the days when I sat in front of the bright lights and camera with the red light signaling we were "On Air." It was the day-to-day stuff I missed-- intensely investigating a hunch, that sense of accomplishment for the stories I wrote and the people I had interviewed. However, I knew that I did not want to leave my children. How then, could I find an equilibrium with this tug-of-war being played inside of my heart?

I began to write in my journal. Ever since I was eight, I have written my feelings on paper. I have a box filled with thoughts scribbled on diary after diary. I love to write. It is as cathartic for me as meditating was for Buddha. So when my mom came up with the idea to write a column for our newspaper about ordinary neighbors who have extraordinary stories, I was intrigued. What a great way for me to be a stay-at-home mom, while also being able to write news stories.

When I approached the editor for our local newspaper, he asked, "Do you think you could find a neighbor to write about each week?"

"Absolutely," I confidently said while concealing my uncertainty. I had no idea whether I could write a weekly column or how long I could keep it up.

So it began. I interviewed each neighbor around 4:30 p.m., when my husband would get home from work to watch the kids. The following day, I would write each article during the kids' nap-time and email the finished copy to my editor. I was a working mom who never had to go into the office. I was able to have my cake and collect my sweet babies' kisses, too.

While I was so happy to have the best of both worlds, I began to realize something. As I conducted our interviews, sometimes I would laugh and sometimes I would cry. But every time-- every time I interviewed a neighbor-- I gained insight. I learned about character. I learned about leadership. I learned about the importance of parents and the harmonious relationships that inspire us all. I realized I wanted to do the same. I wanted to be as courageous as the fire chief and as happy as the three-time cancer survivor. I wanted to be as creative as the inventor and as brave as the retired Brigadier General. I yearned to have the wisdom of the loving mother and the knowledge of the eighty-five year old woman known around the world.

Alas, I cannot be all of those people. I never may likely be. The best way I know how to inspire others as much as they have inspired me is to do what I have done since I was a little girl-- write. So without further ado, here is a glimpse into each neighbor's soul. Each one is special in his or her own right.

THE ESSENCE OF LIFE

Dr. Maya Angelou

If William Shakespeare is hailed as a hero for his poetry and prose, then Dr. Maya Angelou should be considered a "she-ro" for her profound words that evoke a feeling much like the warmth of a hot cup of cocoa on a blustery winter day. As a writer who adores the art of choosing words, I have a deep admiration for Dr. Angelou's ability to do just that. Because her life experiences run so far and so deep, the author seems almost bigger than life. So when given the chance to speak with her, the butterflies in my stomach immediately exercised their wings at tremendous speed. My speech became equivalent to a fifth grader reading aloud in class. I stumbled over my words. I stuttered over my first question. But once I heard Dr. Angelou's calming voice, I was comforted and mesmerized. The hypnotic resonance of Dr. Angelou's voice and her eloquent speech are like a piece of artwork from which one's attention cannot be distracted. Fortunately, she seems graciously interested in telling me about her experiences and about her new book, "Mom & Me & Mom." The story is about how she came to know and respect her mother, Ms. Vivian Baxter, after moving back in with her at thirteen-years old. Dr. Angelou had previously been raised by her grandmother.

Our conversation follows:

You've experienced tremendous hardships and a lot of people would fall victim to that. But you are a glass half-full type of person and have done so well in life. What do you attribute that to?

"I'm very grateful to have been born with a positive attitude and also to have my grandmother, my brother, and mother who were also positive thinkers. They told me I was worth getting up and being resilient. Some people who aren't bound by life or faith are told they aren't worth getting up and so they just fall victim to the news they receive or the bad actions of others around them. But my people told me I was wonderful. I was brilliant.

When I didn't talk for a number of years, my grandmother said 'Sister, Momma isn't okay with these people saying you're an idiot or a moron or something. Momma knows when you and the good Lord get ready, Sister, you are going to teach. You are going to teach all over this world.' And of course, as it turned out-- I mean, she was a black lady of a daughter of a farmer's slave in a little village in Arkansas-- how she could have known that... I went on to teach at the Rome Opera House, to teach at The Hambina Theatre in Tel Aviv. I worked in Egypt and teach in french and spanish. I mean, the main thing is, she told me that, and I believed her.

This is really why I've written this book, Ms. Osborn. It's for parents to say to their children, 'I'm on you're side. Not on the side of the authority. Not on the side of the principal or the teacher or the sheriff or the police officer.' You are on the child's side. You are their support."

It's funny you mention that because my husband tells me I have a hard time saying, "no," to my two-year old son and am always on his side-- even when he throws those famous two-year old tantrums. And I told my husband, "You're so right." I noticed in your book "Mom & Me & Mom" the names by which you called your mother changed. Can you talk about that evolution?

"Yes, when I first went back to her, I was thirteen. I had been raised by my father's mother, my paternal grandmother. She spoke softly. She wore long pearls. She spoke quietly. I went to my mother in California and she had record players. She danced in the kitchen and would sing to the records. She wasn't anything like a mother to me. She said I would have to address her as something. I said she didn't remind me of a mother. She said, 'What do you think I should be called?' I said, 'Lady. Lady, because you are very pretty and you don't remind me of a mother. You remind me of a Lady.' She accepted it and said she would tell everyone she would be called, 'Lady' from now on. She just took it. I liked that in her. I liked that because she was my mother and as an adult, she could've said, 'I want you to call me this or don't call me anything.' But, she went along with it."

My mother once told me that, after her own mother's death, she viewed my grandmother much like an exquisitely beautiful, completed painting, and the more she thought about it, the more nuances and dimensions she saw in her own mother. Did you have that type of experience?

"Absolutely. The older I grew around her and began to appreciate her, the more I was to become a better parent myself. She amused me. At first, she frightened me and I didn't understand her. But I came to really like her. She never laughed at people. She was very pretty. She was young. She had money. But if someone,

3

white or black or Asian or Spanish didn't speak good English or if the person didn't wear nice clothes or even clean clothes-- my mother never laughed at them. You know how some people, when others are out of their presence, will snicker and laugh and make fun of them? My mother never did that. I liked that. I liked that she was fair and generous. So I learned a lot from her."

When you wrote about how your your mom wanted you to shoot the man who almost killed you, I must be honest, I felt as if I could identify because I believe I would have to restrain myself if anyone harmed my babies. I also loved how, when people would tell her "no," she would find a way to make it work. She and I are similar that way-- that good ole reverse psychology works like a charm on us. So what do you think she would say about the book?

"Oh she would love it. She would love it for so many reasons. She would love the fact that I've been very selective. I didn't tell everything I knew. But what I did tell, I told the truth; and she would've counted on me to do that."

What is something about you people may not know?

"Oh I don't know. I mean, I've written thirty-some books. There are two cookbooks, five or six children books, and I'm a poet. I've been at Wake Forest for thirty years and I love it. I came here thirty-one years ago and I feel that I'm a North Carolinian as much as anyone who was born here. I really love North Carolina."

If you could relive one part of your life, what would it be and why?

"I love to dance. The only thing I ever loved was writing and dancing. I studied dance very seriously. By the time I was in my middle twenties, my knees had already given out and so I couldn't continue to dance. I did teach for a while. I loved teaching it and loved to dance, but I couldn't continue to dance. I would've liked to, but obviously the writing fit right in and I was able to begin my career as a writer. That's been a boon to me. That's been my passion. I can understand you, Ms. Osborn, when you say writing is your passion. Nathaniel Hawthorne said, 'Easy reading is damn hard writing.' Just remember that. He said you should write so well that a reader is twenty pages in a book of yours before he knows he's reading."

What advice would you give to others who want to follow in your footsteps?

"Read. To all writers, you need to read. Not only read, but read aloud. Go into your room, close the door and read aloud. Hear the language. Read your own work. Read other works of writers who you think have really touched the Holy Grail. To read aloud, listen to the language and then try to write so well. You know the writer is obliged to take nouns, pronouns, verbs, adverbs, adjectives--- all those bips and baps-- who everybody in the world who isn't a hermit or a mute, uses. Everybody in the world uses words in some language or another. And so the writer has to use this most common thing and make it come fresh-- so that the reader says, 'Oh I never thought of it that way.'"

What sound advice Dr. Angelou passed onto me. I appreciated her offering it without hesitation. While the English language is a course of study learned in all schools, children also acquire precious lessons from their parents as well. Dr. Angelou's mother and grandmother were no exception in providing life lessons for Dr. Angelou. They provided invaluable respect and love that enabled Dr. Angelou to soar. For instance, just like her mother, Dr. Angelou broke glass ceilings-- paving the way for feminists of all kind. Dr. Angelou also became a professor-- speaking to future generations around the world. It was Dr.

Angelou's grandmother who gave that little girl the confidence to know that she could become a teacher.

Both mothers taught Dr. Angelou how to be as mentally formidable as oak. Dr. Angelou believed she could accomplish extraordinary achievements because her mothers believed in her. Perhaps it is gratitude for that intangible asset that led our neighbor, Dr. Angelou, to write her latest book about her mother.

Love your child. Let them know you are always on their side.

Dr. Gary Chapman

Ever hear of a couple driving 400 miles to thank a complete stranger for saving their marriage? It happened to Dr. Gary Chapman. The pastor, radio host, author, and New York Times Bestseller of *The Five Love Languages* said the couple read his book and drove to one of his speaking events. "They told me they never thought they could have love feelings again for each other, but now they do," Dr. Chapman says. These are stories he hears time and time again. While now used to this type of limelight, counseling couples was not a career path Dr. Chapman thought he would lead-- especially considering the rocky start to his marriage.

"When I was in high school, I really sensed I was going to be a pastor-- a preaching pastor. I never thought about counseling or even knew of counseling in those days." As Dr. Chapman studied to become a pastor, he and his wife began to have spats. "I enrolled in seminary two weeks after we got married. Here I was, studying to be a pastor, and I'm struggling in my marriage. I'm telling myself and God there is no way I can be this miserable and preach hope to people." What Dr. Chapman soon realized, is that he and his wife needed to express their love for one another in different manners.

"I needed words of affirmation. Karolyn likes to be loved with acts of service. That's why in the early days we struggled. I didn't do much to help her because I was in school full-time. She didn't give me words of affirmation and I thought, 'If she loved me, she would tell me.' Karolyn thought, 'If he loved me, he would help me.'"

Dr. Chapman began to use his marriage's trials and tribulations as a tool to help strengthen the bond of others who have said, "I do." He began to counsel couples and teach classes on marriage and family. "If we could get back to having healthy families, we would solve many of the social problems in this country because so many of the social problems have their root in dysfunctional families. That is a motivating factor for me and why I spend so much time in this area." Dr. Chapman explains, "I'm not a professional psychologist, it is pastoral counseling. It's basically a gift of God that I developed. I think we all have different gifts. We can't choose what our innate abilities are, but we can develop them."

Another one of Dr. Chapman's gifts, is writing. He began to write what he knew-- which was counseling other couples. His book, *The Five Love Languages,* explains to other people what he teaches in his courses. With the huge success that has followed his book, one might wonder if this pastor feels a sense of pressure to live up to certain expectations of perfection in life and in his marriage. "I can't say that I do because I don't claim to be perfect and in my books and in my speaking I share my struggles. If your willing to be honest and share your own struggles, you don't have an image to live up to." Dr. Chapman reflects, "The crazy thing is, we've all failed. God is willing to forgive us and willing to make things better. That's the message I tell people, 'Life can be better if you trust Christ and allow him to give you the ability to change things.'"

Dr. Chapman explains that he and his wife both decided to be open and honest about their journey to everyone-- a rarity that not many married couples want to make public. "One of the things I found, is when I tell people about our struggles they'll say, 'Whenever you told us about what you went through, that's when I decided this might work.'" Dr. Chapman adds, "You can give all these people your platitudes, but people can identify with struggles."

A hardship Dr. Chapman recently dealt with, was the death of his only sibling, his sister. After eight years, she lost her battle with cancer at a young age of fifty-eight. "What really helped me was the fact that she remained so positive, accepted it, and had the confidence to say that this was ok. In church she always decorated for weddings, but she recruited people to take her jobs." Dr. Chapman says his sister would say in a lighthearted tone, "Alright, I'm going to be gone, so you need to be doing this." Dr. Chapman also mentions, "The way she handled death was helpful. I think walking through the pain of that made me more empathetic of those who have had a death of a family member."

As for advice that Dr. Chapman has for others, he says, "Everybody has struggles through life, but if you have friends who you know care about you, it makes the journey a lot easier. I think the people who don't come out in a good place are those who try to do it on their own. I think it's important to find a group of caring people. It's two-sided. You have the opportunity to help other people. It's the old saying to love and be loved. That's the essence of life and all the rest of it is background music. The heart of life is to love and be loved."

Socrates once said, "By all means, marry. If you get a good wife, you'll become happy; if you get a bad one, you'll become a philosopher." Dr. Chapman has easily achieved both ideas-- a good wife while also becoming a philosopher of love. Our neighbor has put love in his home and in the hearts of the millions of lives he continues to touch.

Put life and love into your marriage.

Love At First Sight

It almost seems like a scene out of the movies. A girl is out with some friends when some Americans in green uniforms walk in. One of them catches her eye and she catches his. There is one problem. She is from Hungary and speaks no English. He is based in Hungary and only speaks English. They both, however, can speak the language of love. "My friend kept translating between us," Timea Reid says in her thick Hungarian accent. "We would dance and smile a lot," she adds with a giggle. "The next day Dylan and I met, we had a Hungarian and English dictionary. It was different, but a good different."

Timea did not expect within a month's time the two would be living together, but they were. "He proposed after three months. I told my friends, he can't be that good, he must be lying, but people can't lie for that long," Timea laughs. The two were shortly married afterwards in an informal ceremony. "I wore black pants and a white shirt." Timea still felt their story was too good to be true and did not want to spend money on an extravagant affair. "I told my mother-in-law ten years ago, I will do a wedding on our tenth year anniversary, until then-- it could be a waste of money." Timea also told her new husband, no children until after five years of getting to know each other. "To see if we would make it," she says.

For the first couple of years, Timea says the secret to their success was the language barrier. That's right, not understanding each other actually helped. "We couldn't fight because I didn't know enough English; and when I would say something, I would mispronounce it and Dylan would just laugh," Timea smiles. What eventually helped Timea with her English, was moving to the United States. For the first six months, she lived with her mother-in-law and learned English. Living with her in-laws proved to be challenging as well as beneficial for her marriage.

"I didn't know what to expect. My mother-in-law corrected my English in every sentence. We had a lot of sit-down talks, but I'm glad I did because I learned a lot about Dylan. Dylan is just like his mom. They don't always say what they mean. I always say it straight. I always tell the truth, whether you like it or not, it's the truth," Timea says with a shrug of the shoulders. "But if I had to do it again, I would, because I learned so much about Dylan."

While Dylan continued to serve overseas, Timea continued to work on her English. "I took English as a second language at Forsyth Tech. Wake was also doing a study where I got paid to go into class and would try to learn the right pronunciation. Then, I would get tested to see what sounds I could hear in various languages." Timea scored a 100 on her test. "They said I should learn as many languages as possible because of my test score, and I said, 'How about I work on my English first?'"

Timea says her ability to listen to the different rhythms and rhymes of the tongue is due to the fact that she has great ears. "One time, I heard the car make a clicking sound," Timea recalls while driving with her husband. She told him to pull over. Dylan did not believe anything was wrong since he did not hear the noise. Timea told him, "I'm serious you should stop." Shortly after, "...the fan came off the motor," Timea laughs with a prideful smile.

With the two lovers cruising right along in their relationship, Timea and her husband decided to have a son. They waited four and a half years instead of five. Their son, Daniel, is now five. With their family well underway, Timea's mother-in-law began to ask when she could hear wedding bells. "My family was going to come to town and Dylan said, 'How about it?'" With forty close family and friends, Timea recently married, or, re-married her husband at a small ceremony at Tanglewood Park. This time Timea decided to wear a long white wedding dress.

As this neighbor continues to make our community and this country her home, her story is proof of love at first sight and the obstacles it can overcome.

Believe in love.

A Hero

As a general surgeon, Dr. Bill Haggerson has often been compelled to stop the bleeding or ease someone's aching pain. When Dr. Haggerson's son, Chris, a 2002 graduate from the United States Military Academy at West Point returned from his second deployment to Iraq, he felt an overwhelming sense to serve his son's comrades and country again. There was a need for skilled surgeons to help wounded Soldiers and Marines deployed in support of Operation Enduring Freedom and Operation Iraqi Freedom. Dr. Haggerson, who served two tours in Vietnam as a bombardier/navigator on an A6 Intruder attack plane, had seen his fair share of war. He also served as a surgeon to finish out his 20 years of service to the Navy, and continued practicing medicine for another 20 years at his practice in Winston-Salem before retiring from private practice at Forsyth Surgical Associates in 2007.

While absolutely admirable of Dr. Haggerson to volunteer his services, it was quite challenging for a man of his age to get back into the Navy. There was little paperwork to be filled out because the idea was an anomaly and Dr. Haggerson was well beyond the mandatory retirement age.

"In 1987, I retired as a Commander from the Navy after 20 years. I became what they call a retired retained. I went on a retired list. It's a ready source in case they need people to serve. But that's not usually done," says Dr. Haggerson. The idea was run by a number of people and continued to be discussed up the ranks. Many were intrigued, but one officer was concerned that it would appear as an act of desperation. The Navy is so desperate that they are now hiring those who are retired? North Carolina Senator Richard Burr's office was contacted for assistance and ultimately the Chief of Naval Personnel signed off on the idea. "I got extended beyond the mandatory retirement age because of the need for surgeons. All that was required was to take a physical, receive orders, and report to active duty." The United States needed Dr. Haggerson, but how did his family feel? Did they not need him, too?

Dr. Haggerson's wife, Dana, says, "When he was in Vietnam, I knew he was in harms way which was hard because I was raising two children alone. But this time, I felt he was a little safer. I don't know if it that was actually true but I always told myself that," says Dana. "It was easier without having little children. It was much easier now that we have e-mail and he can call me."

As for how Chris felt about his Dad being in harms way, he said, "It's kind of a role reversal. When I was in Iraq, I was young. I was naive. I didn't think I could get hurt." Chris begins to get a bit choked up and adds, "but when your Dad goes over there... you worry. You worry about them just like a parent would."

As a parent himself, Dr. Haggerson could identify, "We were concerned while Chris was deployed." Maybe that was one of the reasons Dr. Haggerson wanted to help. Many of those wounded soldiers were sons/daughters, husbands/wives or fathers/mothers themselves. As a trauma surgeon, Dr. Haggerson was the second person to see a wounded soldier. There were Medics, Naval Corpsman and Combat Lifesavers out on the battlefield and then the Soldier or Marine was brought immediately to the area where Dr. Haggerson and his shock trauma team were stationed. Their quarters were surrounded by tents in which the doctors resided and port-o-johns. There were showers, "when they worked," Dr. Haggerson said. The hospital, as Dr. Haggerson describes it, "was a wood structure with wood floors. It's sort of primitive but not too uncomfortable."

As for a typical day, Dr. Haggerson says, "Your primary purpose was to evaluate, resuscitate, and stabilize-- to stop bleeding or if they required surgery, we would do it. Most of the time what we did, was damage control, because we were worried about shock, hypothermia, or bleeding. Then they were airlifted to a hospital in Germany once they were stabilized."

Soldiers were not the only people who received Dr. Haggerson's care. When the President of the United States traveled to Bali, Dr. Haggerson was on the President's medical team who would care for him in case of an emergency. In doing so, the President was assured to receive medical attention from an American surgeon. "I was on the surgical team that went to Bali that supported the President's visit in case something happened and luckily nothing did."

In total, Dr. Haggerson has served four tours in Afghanistan and one in Iraq. His final tour will be aboard, *HMAS Tobruk (II),* in which Dr. Haggerson will be accompanied by two other American surgeons. "It's multi-nation effort to provide humanitarian efforts."

Providing for others is something that Dr. Haggerson will always want to do. While he plans to retire from the Navy after this last tour, Dr. Haggerson is not ready to hang-up his white coat just yet. He is in the process of applying for what's called a locum tenen. He would be on-call as a back-up doctor for local hospitals who are low on staff or need assistance in case of emergency.

Dr. Haggerson says he has gained a lot from the overseas experiences he will continue to use. "It takes a great deal of confidence and you must be decisive when you see a trauma patient. It made me learn to do that. What we do is like what the doctors saw at the Boston marathon. That's what we do everyday. I'm just glad I can help and I'm glad I could serve my country." Although Dr. Haggerson is humble about his continued service, our community leaders are grateful for his contributions.

North Carolina Representative Virginia Foxx said, "You cannot help but be moved hearing Dr. Haggerson's decades-long story of committed service to our country and to troops in need."

The Congresswoman added, "Americans like Dr. Haggerson volunteer to serve when the job is most dangerous and regardless of the price they may have to pay. His drive to give is exactly what sets America apart. Prayers for Dr. Haggerson's safe return to North Carolina and for the speedy recovery of every troop who comes under his charge will be added to my daily prayers for all who serve to protect us."

Heroes do not always wear a cape. They are our loved ones and they are among us.

A Local Celebrity

"Up until eighteen-months old, he was just like my other sons. Then, he somehow lost the words he had learned and stopped having interest in the family," Amy Davis says about her youngest son, Thatcher. "He would only sing, 'Bob the Builder'. He wouldn't respond to his name. He started lining up objects around the house. He wasn't napping and he wasn't sleeping well at night." Amy and her husband tested Thatcher for autism. The test was positive.

"Autism doesn't come with a handbook, so I began researching online about what other parents were doing. We started a gluten-free and casein-free diet. We also got in touch with the A.B.C. school located in Winston. It is one of the few schools in the state that is mainly for autism." Amy says the school has been great for Thatcher, but for Amy it does come with a price. "It was like paying for a college tuition to send him there each year. We were able to send him there on financial aid the first year and then he received a grant from the state that kept him there up until now-

- through his fifth birthday." This year, Thatcher will start public school at Cornatzer. While the teachers will help him at school, Thatcher also has a tutor at home for twelve hours a week, who helps tackle the everyday tasks. He also has occupational and swim therapy. All of these supplemental activities help Thatcher as a whole, but each penny adds up. "It's very overwhelming because insurance doesn't cover it. Plus, it's always the parent doing the research. We may try one-hundred things for Thatcher, but only three things work."

Since Amy understands the stresses of providing financially for an autistic child, she is involved with many fundraisers. "I help with a golf tournament fundraiser in September put on by the Stonger Foundation. I also helped the A.B.C. School raise funds for their financial aid program."

Often times, when others see a special needs child, like Thatcher, they may snicker since Thatcher is not like them. Amy did not want this to happen, especially with Thatcher's two older brothers who do not have autism. So she took action. "When Thatcher has an issue at home, his two older brothers get put on the back burner. So I felt like their classmates at Calvary needed to know what was going on. I asked to talk to each class," Amy explains. "But the principal said, 'no.' He wanted me to talk to the entire school."

For the last three years, Amy has talked to the students in April, during Autism awareness month. "I've had little girls and boys come up to me and say, 'I have a sibling that does that too and I feel the same way.' So Thatcher's brothers are making a positive difference among their peers," says Amy. "And while normally kids would laugh at Thatcher, these students don't. Kids really have big hearts and want to do what's right. They have an amazing ability to cheer on their peers."

With Amy being so vocal about her son's autism, many of her peers seek her advice as well. "The first thing I tell parents is this is not a life sentence. Even though there are really deep valleys, there are really high peaks," says Amy. "Two-- plug yourself in somewhere like the A.B.C. School because they don't just offer classes. They also offer free parent education classes and buddy clubs where your children can come and socialize with non-autistic children. They also do home consultations. Three-- find support groups. Locally, we have the Autism Society of Forsyth County or the I-Can House that's in Winston. It's a place you can go with children of all ages on all ends of the spectrum."

Amy has her highs and lows on her end of the spectrum, too. "Thatcher will always live with us. For others with autism, that's not always the case. It will be for us. Plus, there is the death of a dream that you had for your child-- what they were going to become and what they were going to accomplish. But he's really taught us about humor," Amy says with a smile. "He can be very funny. Thatcher has also taught us the things we thought were once important, really aren't. To see him interact and ask to be with his brothers has been amazing to watch because he didn't do that when he was little. He really seems to draw people in, too." As for being so loving and patient with Thatcher everyday, Amy says, "Without my faith, there is no way I could handle each day. I know his autism is temporary on this earth. There will be a day that I get to talk to him face-to-face and there will be a day that he says thank you... . There are days you wonder why you keep trying, but Thatcher knows I'm trying and I won't ever give up on him."

My interview with Amy has been eye-opening, yielding immense admiration for her devotion to Thatcher. I have a great appreciation for our neighbor who will enlighten anyone who wants to learn about autism and its place in our society. As Thatcher's neighbor, I feel called upon to be as caring as the kids at Calvary, who as Amy notes, "make Thatcher famous" in his corner of our community.

Find a way to give back love to the community from the struggles you have endured. You will help others and you will be rewarded as well.

BEATING ALL ODDS

The Miracle Man

Sixty minutes. About sixty minutes was how long Mike Oswalt did not sustain a pulse. Mike's wife, Sylvie, tried to keep him alive. Her wedding ring on her tightly clamped hands went up and down as Sylvie conducted CPR on her husband's lifeless body. Sylvie kept checking for a pulse as she waited for paramedics. Once the paramedics arrived, Mike received defibrillation, a delivery of electrical shock to his heart. He had to be shocked at least fifteen times in an attempt to restart his heartbeat, which exceeds the typical amount of times a body receives defibrillation. When Mike finally arrived at the hospital, the doctors discovered he had a massive heart attack. Mike's family was taken into a separate room with a Chaplin to help prepare them for the worst. But through what Mike believes to be the power of prayer, he is still alive today. What follows, is the story of his miracle.

Mike and Sylvie Oswalt have two grown children, Alison and Trent, and one granddaughter, Olivia. On the Thursday of the heart attack, Mike had a typical day. He went to work for the company he and his wife own, The Found Alphabet. It features various photographed shapes found in the community that, when combined, create words. But on that Thursday, Mike was showing signs of indigestion and bought a bottle of Pepto Bismal.

"Sylvie and I went to bed around midnight, and I got up and went to the bathroom," Mike says. "Sylvie came to check on me just a minute or two later since she knew I wasn't feeling well. She asked me if I was alright. I said, 'No.'" That's when Mike passed out and Sylvie called 911.

"I couldn't find a pulse," Sylvie says. "But Mike was doing this weird kind of breathing and so the 911 dispatcher said to do compressions. He just kept me going and going and going. He told me exactly where the paramedics were. When they came, I ran downstairs and let them in."

Mike then adds, "I am told they had to shock me fifteen times in the bathroom which exceeds the amount of times they typically shock a person." So why did the paramedics keep working on Mike and not give up hope?

"They would get a blip of a pulse which would give them encouragement to keep going," Sylvie says. "Mike also moaned twice." The paramedics said Mike was hovering over death. Once he was stable enough to commute to the hospital, the doctors were notified and prepared for the worst.

At the hospital, Mike was wheeled into one of the emergency rooms as Sylvie and her two children were taken to a room with a Chaplin. They were told to call close family and friends to possibly say goodbye. Meanwhile, as the doctors tried to save Mike, they discovered plaque built up in the major artery of Mike's heart. The major artery is known as the L.A.D. or the left anterior descending artery. It's the same artery that became occluded and suddenly killed NBC News Washington Bureau

Chief Tim Russert. However, with Mike, the doctors were able to stabilize him enough to do a heart catheterization and put in a stint. Mike's body temperature was then lowered to ninety-one degrees as he was put into a coma to preserve brain cells.

"The neurologist didn't want to give us any false hope because Mike could be fine or completely brain damaged," Sylvie says. The next step was to slowly warm his body and wait. The doctors waited. Sylvie and her children waited. Friends waited. It was during this waiting period that there was an outpouring of love for the Oswalt family.

"Our waiting room was packed with people from church, from the neighborhood, family, and friends. People started to joke that it was like a tailgate party," says Sylvie. "We would gather around together and pray. Our church was praying for Mike. My daughter's church was praying for Mike. There was a Christian radio station in Pennsylvania who asked people to pray for Mike. We were getting emails and texts from people saying they were praying."

Based on the worst-case scenarios the doctors told the Oswalt family to prepare for, it would take nothing less than a miracle to bring Mike out of his coma with the same life he had enjoyed before. In the days ahead, Mike's family and friends would witness firsthand what modern medicine and the power of prayer could do.

In addition to prayer, support came in other forms within the community as neighbors began to learn about Mike's unforeseeable fate. Karen and Mike Lyons live next door to the Oswalt's. Sylvie asked the Lyons to kennel their dog, Maggie. When the Lyons' went to pick up Maggie, they noticed leftover medical supplies lying on the bathroom floor where Mike's lifeless body had been. They decided to clean that up as well.

"No one wants to see that when they come home from a hospital," says Karen. "We didn't do a lot other than try to be a good neighbor," says Karen. As the days went on, the Lyons kept watch over the Oswalt house. When they noticed a lightbulb went out in the Oswalt's front yard, they changed it. While the hearts of many were heavy with the dark situation, the lantern shined as neighbors continued to gather with bright hope and prayer for Mike. Karen adds, "We prayed and just wanted to do any little thing to help them out during that time."

Sometimes, people might be hesitant to reach out to help others in a time of crisis. Not because they don't want to help. Rather, they may not know what to do. The Benefiels, who live down the street from the Oswalts, might have found themselves in just that predicament if they had not taken a creative approach. Being dog lovers, the Benefiels generously offered their home to Maggie so that she did not have to stay in a kennel.

As Tamara put it, "Sylvie is such an organized person and a great cook. I knew we might not be able to rise to the occasion in that way." However, what the Benefiels did feel confident in doing, was providing daily walks for Maggie and giving her a place of honor at night to sleep in the Benefiels' room.

Meanwhile, back in Mike's hospital room, Sylvie never left her husband's side. She slept at the hospital. She showered at the hospital. She ate the hospital food. However, Connie and Tom Meadors, who also live in the Oswalt's neighborhood, rushed to Sylvie's side. They brought her food in addition to other miscellaneous items.

"Mike and Sylvie were one of the first people we met when we moved to the neighborhood. They also go to our church," says Connie. "They are just really special people. They would do the same for us."

Tom concurs, "They are like family; so if something is going on with your family, you are going to do everything that you can just to be there. But I think what we witnessed with Mike was God's hand in action."

The miracle Tom is referring to unfolded slowly after Mike had his heart attack on Thursday night. By Saturday evening, he began to come out of his coma. Sylvie recalls the first moments, "We would say, 'Can you wink?' And he would wink with one eye. Then he would wink with the other--- he's always been a winker. It was shocking because he went from a coma, to barely breathing, to waking up and walking."

What's even more miraculous is that, other than losing twenty pounds in four days, Mike is basically the same person. He does not remember four days prior to the heart attack or a couple of days after. Aside from that, Mike has not changed. One of the first responders on the scene who conducted CPR on Mike is shocked at the outcome. In fact, he had been checking the obituaries for Mike's name.

"There are so few happy endings when CPR happens in the home for that length of time. But everything that needed to go right, did. Sylvie witnessed Mike arresting. She called 911 and immediately did CPR until we arrived," says Adam Berry. "As first responders, we are trained not to get emotionally involved. Yet, it was hard not to be in this guy's corner because we worked on him for so long and he is only fifty-one-years old."

Mike believes the help of the paramedics, his wife, doctors, and perhaps most importantly, the power of prayer, is the reason he is alive today.

"The heart attack didn't change me, but it has been more of an affirmation of our faith. This is such evidence of prayers being answered. People were praying at church, on Facebook, and across the United States," Mike says.

Sylvie adds, "I just feel so grateful to God and to all those who supported us. It makes us want to help others in our situation." Mike agrees.

"We want to take meals to the hospital for others in a similar situation," says Mike. "I've also thought about why God wanted me to stay here-- which can put a lot of pressure on a person. But I don't think I'll ever know that answer. I have always started my day with prayer, saying, 'Please, God, let my heart be open to what you want me to do.'" Mike adds, "A lot of people ask me if I saw a light. I didn't have any experience like that. But today I am more aware of the people around me; and if I want to tell them, 'I love you,' I make sure to do that because I never know what tonight's going to hold."

Mike may not know why he was kept alive, but he did say one girl who lost her father to a heart attack told the Oswalts she now has a renewed faith in God after hearing Mike survived. Mike's story also encouraged my husband, Justin, to take care of his heart. Since my father-in-law had a heart attack at forty-eight, Justin has often expressed concern over genetic problems that may have been passed down to him. Justin eats healthy and since we have a baby and a two-year-old to keep up with, exercising is the last item on the to-do list at the end of the day when we can barely keep our eyes open. But Mike assured us of the need to incorporate both daily exercise and diet for a strong heart. The week after I talked to Mike, we bought a treadmill which keeps my husband's heart healthy as he runs on it everyday for thirty minutes. Ultimately, Mike made us realize it was important to make Justin's health a priority. Now, because of Mike, Justin feels more confident he can be there for our son as he grows from a boy into a man and also be there to walk our daughter down the aisle.

Two months after Mike's heart attack, he is still a walking miracle. In fact, Mike is often seen in his front yard trimming the lawn and spreading pine needles next to the bushes that surround the bright lantern in his front yard-- a common site that many neighbors are so glad to see once more. Another common occurrence for Mike these days is hearing stories from other folks about how his survival has positively influenced their lives. Maybe that is why this neighbor was saved. Maybe it is not what Mike is supposed to do with a second chance at life, but perhaps it is his mere existence that makes him so important. Some might say this neighbor's story is also an example of how a community can come together, and with the power of prayer, save a life.

Never doubt the power of miracles. What you believe you will achieve.

The Optimist

Her laughter is immediately contagious. Aaren Brown's perpetual smile reflects the type of person you want to ask, "What makes you so happy?" Part of the answer may lie in the fact she thoroughly enjoys her job and all the creative opportunities it presents to make a difference in the lives of children. For instance,

if you stepped into Aaren's classroom this year, you might have
seen all of her third-grade students at Southwest Elementary
School bouncing their bums on exercise balls while learning
curriculum that is ordinarily done at a desk. As a a teacher of
eleven years, Aaren likes to think outside of the box-- which means
finding a way for eight-year-olds to extinguish some energy while
focusing on a math problem.

One might even say nurturing children was a calling for
Aaren when she says, "I was meant to be a mom. I would have had
fifty kids, but my husband said, 'no.' I love being around kids,
which is why I am a teacher. I love their humor and what they have
to say about life."

Life, however, has not always been sunny for Aaren. She
has learned to admirably weather some pretty traumatic events. At
twelve years old, Aaren's brother was accidentally shot in the face
by his best friend.

"My mom and I pulled up into our driveway, and police
officers were everywhere. My brother was fifteen and knew to
check the gun for bullets, but one was jammed. He didn't see it.
My brother was shot point blank in the chin. It exited out of his
cheek. If the bullet would have entered half an inch the other way,
he would be dead." As her brother had several reconstructive
surgeries, Aaren went to live with her best friend. The twelve-year-
old quickly began to take on the role of being a supportive adult.

"I had to grow up. I had to take care of myself-- even with
school. I had to help my parents because they were helping my
brother." Aaren then adds with a smile, "But my brother is a police
officer in Kernersville now and his best friend who shot him was
the best man at his wedding." Unbeknownst to Aaren, there would

be more medical hardships to come. She tells me about the moment that changed everything in her world.

"My first son, Chandler, was born on March 25th, 1995." Aaren says during her pregnancy with Chandler everything was normal. Her labor of thirteen and a half hours was normal. But there was one problem. When Aaren delivered Chandler, his flesh was purple. Something was very wrong. "He made one cry and I got it on video. Then, they took him to the NICU. He looked completely normal on the outside, but his liver was in his chest. His heart was on the right side of his body and he only had half of a right lung." Chandler had a very rare birth defect known as a Diaphragmatic Hernia.

Despite the fact that Aaren was still recovering from the epidural given during labor, she says she managed to walk to the Neonatal Intensive Care Unit to be by her son's side. "His oxygen saturation was low. It was at forty. When I walked up to him and he heard my voice for the first time, his oxygen level shot up to ninety-two." Then it lowered precipitously again. Not long after, the doctors told Aaren there was no hope. The nurses unplugged the machines and handed Chandler to Aaren. Chandler then passed away in his mother's arms.

"He lived for ten hours and three minutes. But to me, he was nine months old because that boy was my son as soon as I found out I was pregnant." Aaren dressed her son for his funeral. "I told the guy at the funeral home that there is one thing I want to do and that is dress my baby. I also was the one to put him in his little coffin."

"That changed everything. My husband and I got closer. But seventeen years later, there isn't a day that goes by that I don't wonder what he would've been like. Every year on Chandler's birthday, we let a balloon go. I feel at peace because I know he's at peace and is up there watching his three brothers."

Aaren says, "Even now our family has hardships. My husband had to get his appendix removed and the doctors found out it was full of cancer. If it would have ruptured, he would have died." Aaren adds with encouragement in her voice, "I could easily climb into a hole and just fade away thinking about my problems, but I can't because I have a lot of people who depend on me. I can't let my kids down. I have to be supportive of my husband." Aaren continues, "It's easy to dwell on the bad, but you can't because you will just fade into that black cloud that follows you." Luckily this neighbor chooses to focus on adding a little more sunshine into our lives-- no matter how dark a situation might look.

Behind every dark cloud lies the sun. Find your sunshine.

Conquering Self

When I met Jeremy Wanichko at Starbucks for our interview, he arrived with his little brother and Dad. Jeremy struck me as a mature sixteen-year-old. When he sat down, Jeremy did not send text messages or update his Facebook status on his cell phone. Instead, Jeremy focused on one of two things-- answering my questions or playing with his little brother. His younger brother, who is probably half of Jeremy's size, is entertained. To anyone watching, it is obvious Jeremy has a soft spot for his sibling and vice versa. What is not clear to the eye, are the struggles Jeremy has been through. But after the soul-baring speech Jeremy gave at school, some now know about what he has overcome. If you don't, here's a small part of his story.

It all started in health class at West Forsyth High School. Jeremy and his fellow students were asked to write an essay for the "Rotary Against Drugs" speech contest. The speech would then be judged by the teacher. The six winners would then be considered by some members of the Clemmons Rotary Club. Jeremy won the best speech in the entire school. He would go on to Guilford Technical Community College and compete with fifteen other kids who had won in their district. When Jeremy got on stage, he started out with a poem from www.dailystrength.org. Part of it reads, "I am drugs and alcohol, I destroy homes, I tear families apart, I take your children and that's just the start... ." After the poem, Jeremy went on to say how he has personally been affected by drugs and alcohol.

The teenager said, "My parents were addicted to both drugs and alcohol and it drove my family apart and lead to their divorce. I watched my dad hit my mother many times due to drugs and alcohol-- what they make you do is horrible. For me, it was very hard when I got older. It got worse. My dad started hitting me and I couldn't take it, so I moved in with my mom. She had quit the drugs but was getting drunk every night. I felt like I was on my own, so I started to drink and smoke. It got so out of control, I ended up in the hospital and jail. The things I did with so-called, 'friends,' were the worst choices I ever made. So I quit drinking and doing drugs and moved to North Carolina with my dad after he stopped drinking and doing drugs. My mother still drinks every night. I'm just glad I have one parent who cares about me making the right choices and not being like they were when I get older. I've known many people who died over drugs, but it's too late for them. People still alive can get help and strive towards making a difference."

At our interview, I asked Jeremy why he originally started to take the same path as his parents and he said, "My parents never really cared to interact with me. So I just started to do whatever I wanted to." Then I asked why he decided to change his destiny and how he did it. "I didn't want to go down that road anymore," Jeremy said. "The biggest thing is to find someone to help you and push you through it."

For Jeremy, that was his dad who has been clean for almost two years. Another helpful person in his life is Chris Clodfelter, his marshall arts trainer. "Chris is a family guy. He has kids and is real nice. He's been a mentor to me. I have to keep my grades up or he won't let me train." Muay Thai is a form of marshall arts that Jeremy practices six days a week for two hours. Another passion Jeremy has is cars. He expresses this when talking about his favorite classes. "I like science and I like my career center class, Collision Repair."

But that is how our whole conversation started-- talking about school and his essay. What started out as a simple class assignment ended up stealing the hearts of many who have heard Jeremy speak. And why did he put his personal life out there for all to hear? "Just because I thought it would be good for others to learn about and hopefully make a difference." Jeremy ended up placing sixth at the competition, but it's clear this neighbor will finish higher ranks in life.

Staying silent is easy. Asking for help is the brave path.

The Nurturer

Three-year-old Noah climbs on his mother as if she were a jungle gym. All the while, in the other arm, Lauren Sloop maintains a tender clutch on her seven-month-old, Eli. If Lauren tries to set Eli down, he begins to fuss. Once back in Lauren's arms, his tears dissipate, and Eli's world is sound again by the comfort of his mother's touch. Lauren smiles at each boy and then reaches for her toddler as he begins to slip. Noah is now able to to play on top of Lauren again as Eli speaks the sweet sounds as only a baby can. Any outsider would assume Lauren handles motherhood with ease. However, Lauren will be the first to tell you that has not always been the case.

"I lost fifteen pounds in one month after having Eli," says Lauren. "I felt like I was having a heart attack. I had a fast heart rate. I felt like I was swaying. There was tingling and dizziness-- and it would just come out of nowhere." Lauren was experiencing anxiety attacks. "After my anxiety got really bad, I was having trouble functioning. My parents had to help. My husband, Joseph, had to stay home and help." Lauren recalls, "I was just restless and had extreme panic and worry over everything. I worried constantly that something was going to happen to me. I worried about if something happened to me how Joseph would take care of this newborn and Noah."

During this time period, Lauren and her two sons were also infected with thrush four times in the span of two months. Thrush is a yeast infection that is common in young babies. It can also be easily passed back and forth, thus making the infection hard to eliminate. Lauren said there were days when she felt "hopeless." Everyday tasks became a struggle.

"At my low point, I turned to Joseph and said, 'I feel bad for these boys that I am their mother.'"

Lauren admits she was embarrassed to talk about her struggles. But Lauren knew she must tell her gynecologist about her anxiety attacks. He told her she was experiencing postpartum anxiety. His office only treated postpartum depression. Lauren was told to make an appointment with her regular doctor. Lauren already had a hard time coming to terms with her anxiety, much less finding a babysitter for each doctor's appointment. Nonetheless, she addressed the problem head-on in order to be a better mother.

"My regular doctor told me to take medication. I had a hard time with the idea of medication because I was breastfeeding," says Lauren. "A lot of different medications on the market are fine to take while breastfeeding, but I didn't feel comfortable with that-- which then made me worry about taking the medication that, ironically, is supposed to help me not worry."

For a while, Lauren tried alternative coping mechanisms, such as exercising and therapy. She was told a twenty minute walk could be the same as one dose of medication. "I researched a lot about natural ways that I could deal with anxiety and what vitamins can enhance your mood." Lauren found it was purported that Omega 3, folic acid, b6 and b12 vitamins could help. Ultimately, she decided prescription medication was the best course of action for her which, "...helped tremendously."

Lauren also continues to take other positive steps in her daily lifestyle. "I remind myself everyday of my goal, which is to raise happy, healthy, faithful, children," Lauren smiles. "I have friends with five or six other kids who are doing fine and it is hard not to compare yourself. But I think every mom has a struggle that maybe you don't know about. So I try not to compare and I also try to not demand perfection. Instead, I try to demand some sort of simple improvement-- like getting out of my yoga pants."

Faith, Lauren says, has played a tremendous role in taking back control of her life, as well. "We've always been active in our church. Before we went because we felt like it's what you are supposed to do, but now I enjoy going to church and reading scripture as a family, more so than we did before. I think that's been a blessing, too." She adds, "I know that I am not alone and the Lord did and will continue to help me with all of my trials and struggles as a mother."

As for advice to anyone else who is struggling, Lauren says, "It's not going to go away instantly. Joseph is really good about asking me what I do during the day-- encouraging me to get out." Lauren adds, "I used to look on Facebook and Pinterest and see all these moms who do all this cute stuff and I felt like I should be doing more. I used to wake up and think, 'I need to vacuum. I need to mop. I need to do laundry.' But now I just take it one day at a time. Joseph and I try to consciously talk about the simple things that are important to accomplish each day." Because of these changes, Lauren says she feels more content. "Before, I took for granted being at home and resented that I didn't get to wear my fancy shoes and get dressed up. After going through this, I realize the joy the boys bring into our lives."

Because of Lauren's experience, her family has started a new tradition. "Joseph started this-- every single night, at the dinner table, he asks, 'What are you grateful for?' It's helpful for me to think about what small little blessings there are that day. Then we ask Noah what he is grateful for and what he thinks his little brother, Eli, is grateful for. Even though Noah usually says, 'Spiderman,'-- every once in awhile, he will say, 'Mom and Dad.'"

My mom once told me that all moms need extra love since they are often the biggest dispensers of so many hugs and kisses all day long. It sounds as if our neighbor has found a way to garner happiness and enjoy the time she spends with her children, while creating the loving and nurturing environment she and her husband want to provide for their family. It is an important task. After all, even Spiderman needs a loving caretaker.

You must take care of number 1 before you can take care of number 2, 3, etc. It can be difficult, but you will be better to others if you take care of yourself first.

BUSINESS SUCCESS

The Inventor

Rob never thought of himself as an inventor who could make millions. In fact, when you talk to Rob, he kind of reminds you of Larry the Cable Guy. He looks like he just came in from the backyard after playing catch with his daughter. He sports a plain t-shirt and khaki shorts along with a worn baseball cap. Rob's thick southern accent and endearing manners makes one think, "His mama raised him right." Rob's work ethic is also obvious by his two previous jobs.

"I taught special education children for ten years and mowed lawns on the side for seven of those years to makes ends meet," Rob says. But once his landscaping company began to bring in more business, he knew he had to leave the education system to do what was best for his family. "I loved teaching those kids, but I was making more money in landscaping than I was teaching; so it was just a logical transition."

But a lawn service is not something people need during the winter. Thus, Rob started up another small company called, "Check Up" which helped small businesses re-coup losses from bounced checks. "I would landscape and mow lawns from mid-March to Christmas. From January to mid-March, I would cold-call businesses like doctor offices, dry cleaners, and pizza delivery places to help them get their money back from bad checks," says Rob. Not the typical year-round job; but then again, maybe it is Rob's out-of-the-box thinking that led him to his invention one day in May.

"We had a bad frost the night before when I happened to be cleaning my computer's keyboard with some keyboard cleaner. I sprayed my keyboard and saw it frost over. So I wondered if it would kill the weeds like normal frost does. I sprayed it on some crab grass; and the next day," Rob says with excitement, "the weeds were dead. Afterwards, I tried to recreate the frost. For the next year, I tested out CO_2 canisters and CO_2 fire extinguishers while trying to find out the science behind it. Then my next door neighbor introduced me to Gina Stewart who has a PhD in Organic Chemistry from Chapel Hill. Together, we found that the frost freezes the plant so fast that the plant's cells crystalize with ice, then bursts the cell wall and causes the plant to die. And what's sort of neat is the cell walls in grass don't burst," Rob says with a grin. "We can kill the weeds and not the grass. We are able to use compressed gas to create a cold atmosphere and it is herbicide free."

In layman's terms, "Frostbite" is the first environmentally friendly weed killer and it does not kill the grass. The product is like the frost you see that spreads over the grass on a cold night. Rob describes it like this, "Basically, we are using mother nature against herself to kill the weeds."

Since the idea has come to fruition, the awards have flooded in. "We won the NC IDEA grant, a National Science

Foundation grant, and we are a finalist in the PTP NEXT Grant Competition." Rob says he is looking forward to selling Frostbite. "This is exciting because it has taken four years of a lot of work. But we are finally going to market and hopefully these companies will be happy about it."

The news of his product coming out is spreading like weeds with a long list of buyers already in line. Just to name a few of those waiting: Harvard University, which is an all organic campus; Pleasant Green Grass, an organic lawn company in Raleigh; Good Nature in Cleveland; the Vineyard, the only organic golf course located in Martha's Vineyard; and the Rose Kennedy Greenway Project currently taking place in Boston.

"What a genius idea you came up with," I said to our neighbor.

Rob responds in an almost 'ah-shucks' tone, "It's not genius. So many people tell me it's such a simple idea that it's amazing no one else has come up with the idea first." But no one else has stumbled upon this simply incredible invention or taken the four years like Rob did to perfect it.

Our neighbor's work ethic and invention reminds me of a quote by Thomas A. Edison, "The reason a lot of people do not recognize opportunity is because it usually goes around wearing overalls looking like hard work."

Your imagination never ages.

The Tinkerer

"I was lucky to grow up in that Andy Griffith time period-- when gas was cheap and you could ride around in a 50's chevrolet," Nat Swanson recounts with a twinkle in his eyes and jolly chuckle. His happy laughter is comparable to what I would imagine Kris Kringles would echo, and they are as constant as the snow in the North Pole. Nat, who grew up in Pilot Mountain, is grateful for the era in which he was raised. Nat also feels fortunate that he has been able to spend his time doing what he enjoys most-- being with family and working as an engineer. "I don't think I could ever retire. I'm fascinated by my projects. I'm a tinkerer."

Tinkering since he was a little boy, Nat now owns Security Engineering. The inspiration for his sense of entrepreneurship occurred when he was about twelve years old. At that time, Nat rang the hand bells at his church. One morning while ringing the bells, his family's house caught fire and burned to the ground. Instead of wallowing in the devastation, Nat invented a device that prevented this from happening to other people.

"In the early 60's, we didn't have battery operated smoke detectors, so I started working on inventing one," Nat explains. His creation was incased by an ordinary kitchen utensil normally used for dessert preparation-- a cake pan. He used this because he knew a cake pan could withstand extreme temperatures. The idea panned out and Nat began selling the battery operated smoke detectors to family and friends. As a result, his vision and creation turned into a full-time business.

The same year Nat launched his battery operated smoke detector, a company located in both Denver and Chicago came out with one, too. In fact, Gillette and Sears both wanted to hire Nat and to purchase his battery operated smoke detector. Nat struggled with the idea of selling the fruits of his labor to the big corporations.

Finally, after mulling the proposition over in his head for some time, Nat finally woke up one morning and said, "I'm not going to sell my baby." He had tirelessly worked for other corporations before, and wanted to be in complete control of his destiny by starting his own company. "I decided it would be nice to do my own thing. I think most entrepreneurs luck into things. I've been blessed. I've been lucky with all the relationships that I've had."

Embracing his entrepreneurial spirit allowed Nat to get involved with his other passion-- helping people. In the late 80's, Nat was attending neighborhood meetings and was listening to people express their concerns about putting in a costly town-wide sewer system.

"I realized that the village was going to face an extensive financial burden by building this sewer system. I started to run my mouth and I thought I was getting people elected who supported what we thought. Well, some of the people I supported in the election did a flip-- so we got a town-wide sewer system after all, which was a mistake. Since, I wasn't able to stop the railroading, I felt like I let people down."

The outcome from the sewer system motivated Nat to once again take matters into his own hands. He ran for office and was elected to City Council before serving as Mayor from 1991 to 1996 for the Village of Clemmons. He has since been asked to run for higher offices on numerous occasions; however, Nat was ready to step down.

"I would rather be home with family and support those who are good people." Nat also adds that it was because of family, specifically his wife, Phyllis, that he was elected. "She was a walker. Phyllis went and knocked on everyone's door." Nat recognizes, "She has always been the most important thing in my life, of course. I probably would have been more introverted if it weren't for Phyllis. She has made me an extrovert." The couple has been married for fifty-two years. When asked what the secret is, Nat laughs and says, "Saying, 'Yes ma'am.' I've being lucky to find a good woman. Bless her heart, she's put up with a lot."

Phyllis, who is Nat's devoted wingman, listens as she hears her husband jest about what she has "put up with." Her smiling eyes give a hint of the adoration the two have for each other. While Nat says he is lucky to have found Phyllis, it seems Clemmons is fortunate to have found them both; for behind every good man lies a great woman. And just think how different life would be if Phyllis would have said no to Nat's tinkering. Many lives have been saved because of Nat-- that little boy who wanted to prevent a fire from happening to another neighbor.

Tinker. You never know what you might create.

Racing Through Life

When Steve Sudler goes to a racetrack at the Charlotte Motor Speedway, he is not a spectator. As a Nascar sports marketer, he works with brands such as Farmers Insurance, AARP, Applebee's and Clean Coal. Thus, at the race, Steve is in the garage area working behind the scenes. Originally, however, he wanted to be behind the wheel of the car.

"I grew up in Indianapolis where they have the 500. Racing is big there. I wanted to be a driver, but I wasn't very good." Steve realized he was willing to try anything just to stay involved in the sport. "A really small racing team was looking for a mechanic. I knew enough to be dangerous. So I said, 'Yeah, sure, I can be a mechanic.' I got experience doing the pit stops during the Indy 500 as the gas guy. The driver wasn't a good driver, but he was a good marketing guy and got a lot of sponsors." Learning from his peer, Steve went from pumping gas during pit stops to consulting with various companies about Nascar sponsorships. More specifically, "We look at different drivers, teams, racetracks and we advise companies on where they will get the biggest return on their sponsorship."

In 2005, Steve got offered a position to work with a small agency in Advance to advise Toyota on its sports program. He made the move to Clemmons, even though he would have an office near the speedway. "We looked at places close to Charlotte, but when I wanted to be away from racing, I wanted to be able to be away from the track and spend time with my family."

In 2009, Steve shared in ownership an Indy Car Racing Team called, "Team 3G." The driver was Richard Antinucci. But the cost of operating a racing team got significantly higher. Thus, Steve continued to do what he does best, sports marketing. However, his job has not come without a price.

"I'm very fortunate to have a career in something that I'm passionate about, but it's long hours, a lot of travel and there are sacrifices. I can't tell you how many birthdays, dance recitals, and weddings I've missed. And just because I'm working on the weekend, doesn't mean I get Monday and Tuesday off."

With his profession, Steve can sometimes work seven days a week. Same for Nascar drivers. "One thing I think the average fan misses is the amount of travel that's involved. Going to airports and waiting on flights or having flights canceled-- everyone travels every weekend cross country to go to each race. So, after a race on

Sunday, the driver is usually going to a sponsor function on Monday and a meeting on Tuesday. Wednesday, they might have off, and Thursday is spent preparing to leave on Friday for practice at the track."

Work doesn't stop during the week for Steve and neither does the fact that his kids are growing up. With a ten-year old and six-year old at home, I ask Steve if his schedule causes conflict. "My wife Trisha and I have talked about that and she said, 'You could be at home more, but you would be miserable.' I've been in racing for twenty years, and I've been married for sixteen years; so Trisha knew what she was getting into. My daughter was born in January, and three weeks later, I had to go to the Daytona 500. Owners of a race team don't always understand if you need to take time to see your family."

Yet, Steve is making the best of both worlds, making use of the experience he has accumulated in his career and applying it to his position as President for the youth football league, the Forsyth County Broncos-- a group his kids are very involved in.

"We've done a lot more as it relates to sponsorships. We've looked at ways for the community to be involved other than just contributing a banner. Plus, I get to spend time with my kids at the same time." While Steve may spend a lot of time at various racetracks like the Charlotte Motor Speedway that holds 165,000 fans, it's obvious he likes to spend quality time with his family in our cozy little town of Clemmons that holds a little over 18,000 neighbors.

Hone your gift.

The Fire Chief

"You must be hard pressed for news, if you want to write about me," Chief Jerry Brooks says as I walk into his office at the Clemmons Fire Department. He fires off several people that he believes would be noteworthy alternatives for this column: Mr. Gene Vogler, owner of Vogler Funeral Homes; Mr. Jon Hartman, the General Manager of Vogler Funeral Homes; Jack Higgins who was assistant fire chief; and R.P. Brewer who was fire chief at the Clemmons Fire Department.

"But I am here today to write about you," I insist.

"Those gentlemen have helped me a whole lot through my life. All four have been outstanding to work with and outstanding to work for," the Chief says. Undeterred, I tell him the column is to be about him and his duties at the Fire Department.

"I'm just a spoke in the wheel," the Chief remarks. The wheels in my mind start turning as I see all of the awards hung on the wall-- proof that this modest man has had many irons in the fire. Just to name a few, Chief Brooks has been president and vice president for the North Carolina State Fire Association, president of the Forsyth County Fire Chiefs Council, and president of the Clemmons Civic Club. He received an award for exemplary service from the Rotary Club, and a service award from Clemmons Jaycees that reads, "Whose dedication to service and humanity will serve as a lasting reminder and inspiration to all men of all nations."

While the Chief may not be quick to talk about himself, he is glad to talk about the history of the Fire Station. He explains how those who first volunteered for the Department also had full-time jobs, "Ninety percent of the people here got up to go to work during 1976 through 1978. Some of us were lucky to leave our jobs during the day to go on a call." Lucky? Normally, people run from a fire. Chief Brooks runs to it.

When asked why he first joined the department, the Vietnam veteran said, "It was a good, active thing to join in the community." Chief Brooks became fire chief in 1979 while still working full-time at Vogler Funeral Homes. It wasn't until 1989 that he began working full-time at the Station.

"I like my job. I like coming to work everyday. Some days are longer than others. My job is more administrative than it used to be, but it's got to be done. I've been very fortunate in my life." The Chief's eyes widen and comes in closer almost as if he is letting me in on a secret as he says, "Fire services are a pretty tight brotherhood. When you get it in your blood, you can't leave. This organization has been blessed with good people."

When asked what his family thinks about him going on emergency calls, Chief Brooks talked about the hardships of leaving family behind during bad weather. "I think sometimes people forget when we are dealing with severe weather, we are leaving our families at home. But people know when they dial those three magic numbers, 9-1-1, we will be there." When referring to his wife and daughter, Chief Brooks smiles. "They've been very supportive. My wife is a retired nurse and my daughter grew up in Clemmons. Clemmons is our home." He then talks about Clemmons as a whole.

"This is a blessed community. I say that at least twice a week. We have an extremely good mix of folks. Some are more challenging than others, but generally, everything shakes itself out of the bush alright. The gray area becomes clear. But I'm blessed and privileged."

Elaborating on his family life, the Chief recalls his childhood. "I had a unique experience. My parents moved in with my grandparents. My grandpa was a blacksmith and had a lot of influence on what I do. My grandpa said, 'You work hard and treat people fair. If people need help, you help them.'" Then Chief Brooks referred to Jack Higgins again, the former assistant fire chief, who died two years ago. "He was a very good mentor for me. He taught me a lot. He was a very quiet individual and did a lot of positive things for this community. Things that people didn't know. He had a big heart."

"Is that how people would describe you?" I asked.

"No," Chief Brooks answers immediately. But I'm not buying it. The awards on the wall show differently. He is, in fact, the type of Clemmons neighbor who will always put himself in the line of fire if it means helping or saving someone else.

Be a leader others can look up to and respect.

Finding Fate

It all came down to one test. One test would decide whether Frank Caruso would join the New York Fire Department or continue to study medicine and become a Physician's Assistant. Frank, who was born and raised on Long Island, had always dreamed of joining the Department. After all, he had been a volunteer since he was a senior in high school. But while waiting to join the Department full-time, Frank had begun medical school. Studying medicine proved to be more difficult than Frank thought. Thus, when the Department called him and said they wanted to hire him, Frank had to make a decision.

"I decided if I passed my anatomy exam the next day, I would stay in the medical program. If I failed, than I would go and work for the New York City Fire Department," Frank says with a thick Long Island accent. Then he adds with a big smile, "I passed the test." Frank says that it's interesting that fate dealt him that hand, because soon after, he met his future wife in medical school.

"I met my wife over a dead body," Frank laughs. "She was studying to become a nurse practitioner and was working on a cadaver. But I didn't go out with city girls, so I didn't ask her out until later." Why didn't he go out with city girls, I asked.

"She was from Brooklyn, Jill," Frank grins. "You never know if those girls are going to be carrying guns or what they will do to you," he kids. But Frank's wife proved to be harmless, and their relationship sparked what would turn out to be a perpetual flame.

Staying in school may also have been lifesaving. Frank believes he could have easily been in one of the Twin Towers during 9/11. "My wife says if I would've gone into the Department, I probably wouldn't be here. I knew a lot of those guys who died. And you know, I have a funny feeling that my name would've been on that list of firefighters who died."

Instead of being one of the firefighters volunteering on 9/11, Frank helped in another way-- as part of the medical personnel. He has also helped with Katrina victims, as well as in other major crises situations. That's because he volunteers as the Deputy Commander of North Carolina's Special Operations Response Team. It's an organization comprised of volunteers who assist in major disasters. Plus, Frank is a volunteer firefighter at the Clemmons Fire Department, in addition to his day-job-- being a Physician's Assistant at Wake Forest Baptist Medical Center. So how did this born-and-bred New Yorker end up in North Carolina?

"Someone heard me give a lecture and recommended me to my current boss, here in North Carolina. I'll tell you, my boss, he's a smart boss, because he asked me to bring my wife down to the interview," Frank explains. "During the interview, my boss' wife took my wife around and showed her the schools and the area. After the interview, I told my wife I thought North Carolina seemed nice, but I didn't know if it was worth uprooting our kids. I didn't think I was going to take the job. My wife said, 'Oh yes you are.' So we moved," Frank chuckles. Frank and his family have now been here for a little over a decade.

"It's funny, because I always thought of myself as a coastal guy. I never thought I would be this far inland." But like many North Carolinians, Frank makes regular trips to the beach. In fact, he and his wife just bought a beach house at Oak Island. "We just got the house two weeks ago, and I already talked to the Chief at the Fire Department. I figured if a fire or something is going on, I'll have to see what's happening and will want to utilize my skills." Volunteering is obviously very important to Frank, which is why he is also a Eucharistic Minister at Our Lady of Mercy.

"The Church and Fire Department really established my dedication to the community. My father who came to Long Island from Italy didn't understand why I would volunteer my time and not get paid. But I think it's important to do that, and I have tried to raise my kids to do the same."

With all that Frank does, we are lucky fate intervened, helping him pass that one test during medical school. While he would have undoubtedly made an incredible fireman for the New York Department, our Clemmons neighbor has been a valuable asset to our community and to others around the United States.

Don't question your fate. Follow it.

The News Anchor

After a stretch of the arms and a nice long morning yawn, many of us will pour our first cup of coffee, switch on the TV, and listen to the top news headlines of the day. One person who delivers our news just also happens to be our neighbor, Kimberly Van Scoy of WXII. While thousands of people enjoy Kimberly's company as they start their day, it seems ironic that Kimberly considers herself somewhat shy by nature.

"No one really believes me when I say I am shy," Kimberly says with a smile. "But when I get in front of big crowds, I get nervous." In front of the camera, though, her fears fade. Kimberly shines. Most likely, it is because of her passion for news. "I've been at the forefront of huge stories and it has given me an incredible window into the world. I've met people at the height of happiness and the depth of despair." The fast-paced environment, the constant deadlines, and working under the axiom, "the show must go on," seems to be a thrilling adventure for Kimberly. However, Kimberly had originally intended to go to nursing school.

"I became a journalist by accident. I had enrolled in nursing school and got a job in radio. Then I caught the broadcasting bug. I was doing radio news and a TV news director heard my voice and called me." Kimberly then began working for the CBS news station in Memphis, Tennessee, and never looked back.

After Memphis, Kimberly worked in other various states, such as Anchorage, Alaska, and Boise, Idaho. She finally settled in

North Carolina at WXII in 1998. "There's a really good sense of community here. In Winston, you have the mountains, the beach, and everything is close by. Our family is close by, too." At a recent trip to the beach, Kimberly's family helped her conquer a fear.

"I have a fear of water. I will go in a swimming pool, but I won't go into a lake or ocean. I've done too many shark stories on air. But last year, I had a big girl moment. My family and I walked out in the ocean and the water came up to my waist. My heart was racing the whole time," Kimberly says with a giggle. As youthful as Kimberly looks, some people may be surprised to learn that she is also a grandparent-- a job that is not without its opportunities for humor. Kimberly admits she did not want to be called Grandma when her first granddaughter was born. She decided on the name, Nana instead. That name has since been changed, courtesy of her granddaughter.

"My granddaughter can't say Nana, so she calls me Bananas." Kimberly also spends time exercising, scrap-booking, gardening and volunteering. She helps out at Hospice and is involved with the Free to Breathe Walk, which helps raise money for Lung Cancer. Since her mother mother died of lung cancer, Kimberly says the program is near and dear to her heart.

Her big heart and compassion for others is probably why Kimberly vividly remembers covering one particular story in 2008. "The tornado happened on Frye Bridge in Clemmons. It was interesting because I was the first reporter on the scene and there were literally houses teetering on their foundations. I interviewed one family who hid in their closet, and their house was gone. Seconds count in that situation and they are proof of that because they would have been dead if they would not have taken shelter in the closet," says Kimberly. "It's interesting to talk to those people because they thrive in situations like that. I have no knowledge of what it would be like to lose everything. I have some of my fathers World War II medals and I can't imagine losing those," Kimberly tells me. "I went back and interviewed the woman a year later, and I was so impressed with how well she had picked up and moved on." Stories like those are what motivates Kimberly to get up as early as she does to deliver the news.

"I'm up at 2:00 a.m. and at work by 3:00. I'm awake. I don't know how I am, but by the time I am on air, I am awake." As we enjoy what may be our second cup of joe while Kimberly is center stage in front of the bright studio lights, it is nice to know we are getting our the first breaking news of the day from our neighbor. And while it can been said in many instances that no news is good news, in this case, I would say our neighbor has a good story worth telling.

Live your life so fully that it is newsworthy.

The Dreamer

Mickey Mantle, Dean Smith, and Elizabeth Taylor are just a few of the people Captain Bill Marion has met during his career. Coming in contact with such celebrities is a big deal for some, but Marion is modest.

"If you fly as an airline pilot, you meet a lot of people," Bill explains. Becoming a pilot for Piedmont Airlines was not something Marion ever dreamed was a possibility. Growing up in Surry County, Bill was raised by a tobacco farmer. The only pilot he ever knew was a crop-duster. Instead of following in the family footsteps, Bill branched out and worked at Reynolds Tobacco.

However, he was very unhappy. Then, as "good fortune" would have it, a co-worker asked Bill to take a flying lesson.

"During the lesson, I was a nervous fool. But for some reason, I went back." Over the next year, Bill took to the skies as Jacques Cousteau took to the seas. "I had a tremendous desire to become a pilot and I believed I could. Once I decided that I would start flying, I went after it with all my might." For Bill, chasing his dream meant buying an airplane in order to get as much practice as possible. With two small children at home, the purchase was a financial risk for his family. "I bought an airplane for $900," Bill recollects with humor. "I borrowed every penny of it from the bank. I was afraid to tell my dad. My little boy spilled the beans on me to my dad, who then told me I needed to take the plane back and get a refund."

Bill's burning desire to become a pilot defied all logic. In fact, he even enrolled in the grounds school at Piedmont. The grounds school already had a full class of pilots. Yet, they always accepted local pilots with little experience like Bill, in case one of the more qualified pilots dropped out. There was one drawback. The three-week class took place during the day. Bill worked during the day. Undeterred, he asked if he could work the night-shift.

"Reynolds said I could work nights only if I took a salary cut and went back to the salary they gave me when I first started nine years earlier." Bill accepted the offer, which eventually paid off. A pilot dropped out. Bill was hired, and he was off to a flying start.

Bill quickly soared through the ranks, eventually piloting international flights on Boeing 767's and retiring as Captain. He believes, "You need to find a vocation in life that you really enjoy. You can work harder when it is something you love than if it's just another job." The retired pilot adds, "There are things that come and go in your life that are out of your control... you think you are in control of your life but you are not. I was lucky enough to have one of those pilots drop out." Bill adds, "Because I became a pilot, my wife and I got to fly to places and see things we never could have dreamed of. We have vacationed in St. Thomas, hiked in Switzerland, and gone skiing in Austria." While Bill enjoys talking about his good ole days, the person he speaks of the most is the real love of his life-- his wife, Carlene.

"I'll tell you, my life wouldn't have been the same without Carlene. It took me a while in life to realize how wonderful she was. When you're young, you don't always realize the good things." Bill's wife, who passed away from cancer in 2006, is still very much a part of his everyday thoughts. They were married for nearly fifty years. Bill shows me pictures of he and his wife. Their body language is telling of the bond they shared-- always grabbing each other's hands or posing with their arms around each other. "She was one lovely girl. Absolutely, knock-down, drag-out gorgeous." Bill also brags about what a great tennis player his wife was and how they enjoyed the sport together. He says she was always very supportive of him. "It was almost like she devoted her life to me; and by doing that, I did everything I could to make her happy."

Living a happy life is something this neighbor can proudly say he has accomplished. "I would say I have had as good a life as anyone who has ever lived. I had a wife and job that I dearly loved. Can't get much better than that."

Too often we are on autopilot and go through life not achieving our true dreams. Our neighbor, Captain Bill Marion is a great reminder that the sky's the limit.

Believe in yourself and aim even higher than the stars. Do not hold yourself back.

The Chief Deputy Sheriff

When my mom was a little girl, she kissed her father goodbye and told him to be safe. She knew when my grandpa put on his uniform and badge, he was willing to put himself in the line of fire. While it scared Mom, it was a life my grandpa loved to lead. That life is also the one Forsyth County Chief Deputy Brad Stanley chose, too.

"It's always been a career that I've enjoyed. I hear many people talk about *having* to go to work. But I enjoy going in early and staying late," Brad says with a grin. "It is that personal satisfaction of hoping my part is making life better for someone else." Brad, who is second in command under the elected Sheriff Schatzman, says his job is not just about catching the bad guys.

"It's also about community. We want everyone to understand that law enforcement is there for everyone in the good times and bad. Law enforcement is a steward of the community." The Chief Deputy is as dedicated to the six-hundred employees that he supervises as he is to the citizens of Forsyth County and its economy. "Our budget is just over 43 million dollars. We are always looking for better ways to improve what we do for less money since we use the tax payers money-- especially with the economy the way it is."

Likely Brad's attitude of striving to do better has contributed to his success. In 1998, he was Officer of the Year and was one of five outstanding public servants recognized in the state of North Carolina. In 2003, he became Lieutenant of Internal Affairs. In 2006, he completed a leadership program in which few applications are accepted. The three month course is headed by the F.B.I. and includes physical training conducted by the Marines in Quantico, Virginia. In 2009, Brad was promoted to Major of the Law Enforcement Bureau. Last year, he was promoted to Chief Deputy. It seems Brad has a true aptitude for his occupation as well. His old partner says the Chief Deputy always has a knack for finding the bad guy.

"It seems when something wild is about to happen, I'm always in the area," Brad puts his head down, chuckles, and looks up as he says, "My old partner used to tell me that if I was sitting in a parking lot, a drunk driver would find me and run into my car. I'm just lucky to be where the crime happens."

Brad says his job is more than just being in the right place at the right time. "You have to build rapport. We are usually dealing with people on the worst day of their lives. So yes, a person has committed a bad act, but they are still a person. If you build rapport, you can figure out what has contributed to to this person committing this crime. If you can get to that point, you can help this person get help and also help others in solving the case." Brad says he identifies with the fact that, "We are all human and that is something we have to remember. We are all going to make mistakes - even me."

For someone who seems so compassionate and high-spirited, I ask how he doesn't take his work home with him. "You do. But in order to be a successful person in dealing with the good and the bad, you have to find ways to deal with that through faith, family, or friends. I would think it could eat you alive if you don't deal with it. I have two dogs, a black lab and a cocker spaniel. It's a good way to escape because they are always happy to see me."

His philosophy sounds familiar. Likely it resonates because my grandfather was the same way. He always seemed happy to see us and handled whatever came his way with humility, compassion, and humor. Quite possibly, that is also because he loved his job. In fact, my grandfather said, "If you love your job, you will never have to work a day in your life." Brad agrees. "If everyone chose to behave themselves and the world didn't need law enforcement anymore, I don't know what I would do. I don't work for the money, I just love what I do."

I thank our neighbor for putting himself in the line of fire, putting the community first and his life last. Just as my mom wished for my grandfather, I hope for our neighbor to stay safe on his job.

Handle life's experiences with humility, compassion, and humor.

The Barber

Before I walk into the oldest barbershop in Clemmons, I see the striped barber shop pole swirling around, signifying a barber is available. Once inside, I take one step, maybe two, before being greeted by the jovial Barber Terry Brown. Smiling back, I scan the shop and feel as if I have stepped into the 50's. Sandy blonde hair clippings rest under a black chair. A boy sits still as Terry skims his head with a hair clipper, making a buzzing noise. The father, who looks as if he is sporting a fresh buzz-cut himself, glances at a magazine while waiting for his son and chatting with Terry.

"I'm a people person," says Terry who has owned the shop for the last four years. "I had a a great uncle who was a barber. There was also a barber in Mocksville I really looked up to named Nelson Jones." Then with pride in his voice, Terry, adds with his contagious laugh, "But, I'm the only one in my profession that is an ACC barber. I worked near Wake Forest, N.C. State, and Chapel Hill."

I tell Brown that I went to N.C. State. He replies, "I used to cut Philip Rivers hair," a former N.C. State quarterback who now starts for the San Diego Chargers. "But for me, I've always believed in hard work and I always try to treat everyone the same. I don't care if you're an NFL quarterback or the janitor of a school, if you are a good person, that's what matters to me."

Terry then starts laughing his belly laugh in anticipation of his next story-- a common trait of Terry, which ends up making a person laugh before they know what the joke entails. "There was a fellow who came in and he was very excited about this new car he bought. It was a Lincoln. While cutting his hair, he kept telling me how this car was just the best," Terry grins. "After we were done with his haircut, he left but came back five minutes later. He said, 'There's something wrong with my car.'" Terry cracks up, "He had a keyless car entry-- which was a first during that time. He said, 'I can't figure out how to get into my car.' For thirty minutes, we were sitting out there trying to get into the car. He had the dealership on the line while I'm pushing all the buttons on the keyless car key. I guess I hit the panic button, because the car alarm went off."

Terry pauses his story because he can not contain his infectious laughter. "A car four or five spaces down had its alarm go off. We had been trying to get into the wrong car."

Laughing with Terry, I'm not surprised that he has regular customers who come from out of town to get a haircut. "I have a lot of customers who travel for business who are from Raleigh and Charlotte. When they pass by town, they come to me."

"Why did you come back to your hometown?" I asked.

"I am from Davie County originally and wanted to come home. I am a community-based person and I like being in a place where you can build relationships with people. At the Universities you can't do that. But now I'm home where the community here pulls together and cares about one another. It's genuine. This is God's country," Terry tells me. The extroverted entrepreneur also tells me where he got his personality from.

"My parents. Mom and Dad had a great sense of humor and had very outgoing personalities. They taught me that humility pays off. I always try to be a positive, outgoing person." Terry continues, "If you have a dream chase it. If you put your faith in God, you'll always win."

Luckily, Terry's dream landed him back in Clemmons. Having him as a neighbor makes Clemmons feel like a town who is living in the twenty-first century, but has the open-armed mentality of the fifties.

Laugh a big belly laugh everyday.

The Shy Student

If you are like me, you like many things about coffee -- the fresh smell, the swishing, swirling, sound of it poured into a cup, and the sensation of the dark liquid as it warms your body. Then there is the caffeine aspect of it. Without my java, I turn into a lion growling at those who cross my path. Well, maybe I don't get that surly; but occasionally, I do find myself in need of an extra pick-me-up. In that case, I go to Starbucks. The hustling and bustling of the store in Clemmons with its steaming coffee, is almost like a caffeinated version of the show, "Cheers". It's a place where everybody knows your name.

"Hey, Jill. The usual?" I hear as I walk up to the counter. The person on the other side is a familiar face. Her name is Sherrie Richmond. She has her hair whipped back in a ponytail. She is taller than most girls, very smiley, and seems genuinely glad to greet people.

"Yes," I smile, impressed that she remembers my name and order.

"How is your day going? Did you have a good week?" the gregarious Sherrie consistently asks me when I step into her office.

"Great. Can we get together, so I can ask you some questions for an article?" I ask.

"Why not," she says with a smile handing me my mocha. With her personality, I know there is more to this Clemmons neighbor.

So here is what I found out.

The bubbly Sherrie, who is in college, admits she used to be very sheepish and shy.

"I couldn't even talk to a guy customer without blushing or turning red," Sherrie says with a smile and nod confirming the statement. "Eventually, I began to learn that people like when you say, 'Hello'. I think that's the biggest thing, is not worry about what you look like-- tall, small, or skinny-- just be yourself. Just talking to someone makes all the difference in the world." Sherrie also tells me she is a student at Forsyth Technical Community College and plans to go to Salem College in the spring.

"With the economy, a lot more people are going to community college and paying a lot less to take basic courses. Then you can transfer and focus on your specific undergrad courses at a university." At Salem, Sherrie plans to major in biology. Next, she wants to go to medical school and become a doctor in oncology pediatrics. In this emotional field of helping children with cancer, Sherrie hopes to use her vibrant personality to help enliven sick children.

"If I were a patient, it would put me at ease if my doctor was more friendly. A patient wants to be treated medically, but you don't want to be treated differently as a person. I think as a doctor, you need to get to know the person, not just their chart." Sherrie believes that, "There will be the bad days and the hard times, but I think the most rewarding thing will be the fact that I have helped people. It will have its positives and negatives, but that's just life."

When referring to an internship she had at Baptist Hospital, Sherrie talked about a woman in the Intensive Care Unit who did not have any visitors. She said, she made an effort to say hello and the importance of that human connection. "Even if you go in and talk to someone and they don't know you, at least they are being talked to. It's not how long they are here for, but their quality of life. Just talking to someone as a friend can make a difference."

Then I ask Sherrie what she likes about Clemmons. "It feels like its own tight knit community. One specific customer came in the store right after his mom died. He said he didn't know where else to go, because he felt like our store was like family," Sherrie says.

After sitting down and talking to Sherrie, I can see why this man would be comforted by surrounding himself with someone like her. After all, this neighbor is warm, comforting, and gives you energy. Almost like a fresh cup of coffee.

A "Hello," served with a smile, can make a person's day. Try it.

The Teacher

In the halls of a high school, life is vibrant. The energetic teens are infectious. But, it isn't just the teens that lend spirit to the gymnasium and classrooms. If you happen to run into Ms. Russ, the Civics and Economics teacher at West Forsyth High School, you get the same vibe. Petite, with an effervescent smile, her fun personality fills a room. It is clear why teaching is the perfect profession for Kirstin Russ.

"I always wanted to be a teacher." She continues, "I love to learn and there is not a better profession. Teaching involves phenomenal energy and it's a great outlet to use energy. You always have to think on your feet." Kirstin says, "It uses my love of energy, my love of creativity, and my love of learning. The kids change and the situations change and you have to keep up with both." Kirstin sets high standards for herself and her students.

"I base myself not by what the students get in the classroom, but if they can apply what they learned in the real world." She tells her students, "You had better get out to vote and speak your minds, because you do make a difference."

When asked if there was a favorite moment while teaching, Kirstin answers, "I had a student one year who wasn't sure about school. So I nicknamed him, 'Brain.' I used him to help other kids in the class. Later, I got an email that said, 'Hey Ms. Russ, this is Brain. I stayed in school and went on to community college.'" That certainly is rewarding.

Kirstin, who has lived in Clemmons since 1996, says, "We were not looking to move to Clemmons, but there was a house perfect for our family with a tire swing and basketball goal and treehouse in the back. The community had a good family feel about it." She gives an example of how other families help each other.

"One time, my child was lost and I was terrified. There were six different neighbors who came out to help me. And that's a really nice feeling. That neighborhood support is amazing." Then I ask where her son was, thinking how horrified I would be if I lost my son. She tosses her head back and laughs in disbelief, "He was playing at a neighbor's house who had not answered the phone when I called."

"Usually we are locked in our own life, but people come out to help. We have our differences and that is human. But I feel like the bottom line is that everyone in Clemmons tries to better our community."

Hearing Kirstin, reminds me of a lesson that my dad taught me when I was little. We were in a bright red canoe and had stopped paddling for a brief rest. He said to me, "Look, Jill," and flaps the oar in the water. Then he stops and silently sits the oar in his lap. "Look at how just one person can create those ripples. One person can affect so many." Kirstin is doing the same. This neighbor is creating positive ripples in our community of Clemmons, one child at a time.

Find a career that energizes you.

The Vet

Kinkachoos, chinchillas, iguanas, owls, and tortoises are just a few of the exotic animals that can be found at the Animal Ark. Dogs and cats are barking and meowing in the waiting room too, but veterinarian Mitch Spindel says that a lot of injured animals found from our everyday neighbors are brought in as well.

"We've had swans, ducks, and geese from Tanglewood who were brought in after getting bit or hit," Mitch says. "We've also built prothesis for a number of tortoises. There are a lot of tortoises out there with blue fiberglass shells. Maybe I should start signing their backs," he jokes. Mitch says he has always loved animals and knew he wanted to become a veterinarian when he was six-years old. "Most six-year olds wants to be a vet, but my cousin, Ed, who is fifteen years older than me became a vet and opened an Animal Ark in Syracuse. So I followed in his footsteps." Mitch decided to open up his own Animal Ark in North Carolina and made the inside look almost like a spa. It has a sense of tranquility inside and yet a sense of character on the outside

"I visited one-hundred and fifty hospitals to see how I wanted things to flow inside our office," says Mitch. "My friend said he could build a boat outside in the front and we kept brainstorming on silly ideas. However, I did draw the line when my wife suggested we buy the giraffe from Putt Putt when they were going out of business," Mitch chuckles. As the Animal Ark was eventually created in Clemmons, Mitch made sure to bring the same values that Cousin Ed had instilled in him.

"Take good care of the people around you and they will take care of you," says Mitch. "I hire bank tellers and check out clerks-- I hire nice people, not necessarily the most experienced. I also give them the ability to make their own decisions. It's important to surround yourself with good people who want to be here because then they go above and beyond for the animals."

Mitch seems to do same for the community as his staff does for their furry clients. Mitch was a board member for the Dog Park Committee. He is Chairman of the Building Committee for the Forsyth Humane Society. "My job is not to raise the money, but to spend it on the new facility we are building-- which is more fun than asking people to donate money," Mitch says with a smile. He is also the president of Forsyth Veterinarian Medical Association. "It's a way for about seventy vets to get together. It's a really good thing that most counties don't have. It's also a way to have continuing ed and camaraderie between all the vets in the community."

Another one of Mitch's hats is being a board member of A.R.F., the Animal Adoption Rescue Foundation. "I helped design and implement an in-house veterinarian clinic for their animals. So every Thursday night, anyone who fosters an animal for A.R.F. gets free veterinary treatment for their animals." He's also a board member for Humane Solutions and helps raise money to educate people on spaying and neutering.

"What do I get out of this?" Mitch asks. "I've got wonderful relationships with animal people. It's just good be to be connected." Mitch adds with a laugh, "And with all that, I don't think I have a junior vet in my house. I have four kids-- thirteen and older at home-- not one says they want to be a veterinarian. But that's ok. Family is a big part of my life-- keeping up with my three boys and daughter can be a challenge, especially since the boys who are in middle school and high school are bigger and stronger than I am now. But," Mitch laughs with a gleam in his eye, "I can still take away the car keys."

Seems as though this neighbor is is in the driver's seat when it comes to helping the animal community. His passion for others and animals seems like an instinct that could never be caged.

Explore your wild side and help rescue an animal.

The Rock & Roller CEO

He is the Senior Vice President and Chief Operating Officer for Forsyth Medical Center by day and a rock-and-roller by night. Paul Hammes is the lead guitarist of the band, The Hold Up, by night. The six-man band is composed of Clemmons residents who play songs from the 70's, 80's and 90's. The high energy, gregarious, Paul grew up in Athens, Georgia, a place he tells me is big for music.

"The B52's came from there and R.E.M, to name a few," says Paul who is dressed in slacks and a light blue buttoned up shirt. Paul may appear professional, but he can not help but grin a bright white smile while explaining his musical inspiration.

"I took guitar lessons from a nun in 6th grade at school. After a year, I stopped. In high school, I bought my first electric guitar which was the equivalent of a canoe paddle with knobs on it. I basically taught myself by ear. I played on and off through college. When I would play, I would forget everything around me. It was very cathartic." That explains his introduction to and interest in playing guitar, but how did he end up as a hospital administrator?

Flashback to Paul at nineteen-years-old when he found himself working as a unit secretary for a hospital in Athens. "It beat selling hot dogs on the corner and it was one step above working in the laundry mat-- my job before that," Paul laughs. "The secretary job was very informative for me because I got to see what it's like to be a patient in a hospital and what it's like to be a part of a team when people come to you at their most vulnerable stages. I got to see people when they celebrated good news or very bad news. You either fall in love with that environment or it's not for you. I felt like it was calling."

Well, that answers how Paul found a career in the field of patient care. Now how does he account for his rise from unit secretary to overlooking 4,000 employees? He said after he graduated from the University of Georgia, he realized, "I've always been fascinated by what motivates people to perform above their own expectations." Paul went on to get his M.B.A. at UGA while also serving in the Georgia Army National Guard. It was there Paul realized he loved helping those around him.

"In bootcamp, something awakened within me to want to become a leader. I found successfully leading a team through difficult situations was personally rewarding."

Upon graduation, the hospitals were contracting and Paul went to work for Cintas, a company that provides uniforms for other companies. One day, while in the office, Paul got a phone call that one of his delivery people was sick. It fell on Paul's shoulders to pick up the slack. Thus, he drove the truck and delivered the boxes full of uniforms to each address. Being the one to provide service to customers as well as do any necessary backbreaking work gave Paul a clear outlook of the importance of frontline service-- a lesson he has brought with him today to the hospital.

"From the patient's perspective, it is about the people at the bedside and meeting each patient's unique needs in a way that is special and memorable." Although Paul is in charge at Forsyth, he says it's not about him.

"My role is to provide resources, remove barriers that might exist, and to aim and align the team. I believe leadership is about everyone but you. Our employees are the ones at the front providing the service. I work for our employees."

It might surprise those employees to learn their boss has a night gig in a band. It's a spotlight in his life that Paul himself never expected to have at this point in his life. After all, he has plenty of other activities to fill his time. Paul serves on the Board of Directors for the Northwest NC YMCA, Piedmont Regional Trauma System (PRTS), the Arts Council of Winston-Salem/Forsyth County, and is Vice Chair of the Forsyth Technical Community College Foundation Board of Directors.

Sounds like you might need the energy of a superhero to keep up with that kind of schedule. If you could, you might even get a big head about it. But not this neighbor. Paul stays well grounded... on stage with his electric guitar.

Dare to be different.

A Piece of Cake

When making a cake, most of us buy a box of mix at the store. We throw in some eggs and water, then toss the gooey batter into the oven. Afterwards, we slather on some icing and call it a day. Not David Binkley. That method is too simple. A piece of cake, if you will. David has decorated cakes as tall as six feet high and cakes that have extended up to eight feet long. If you worked at Dewey's Bakery for forty-seven years as David did, you would be bound to get some large cake requests. Literally. But David never imagined he would be working at a bakery for that long or that he would be decorating cakes. He just sort of fell into it.

It all began after high school. A friend notified David that Dewey's needed a delivery truck driver. David interviewed and got the job. In between deliveries, David began to help ice the cakes.

"I delivered for ten or fifteen years, and I started to help ice the cakes a little bit... and then a little bit more." With no formal training, David's natural talent became evident. "I always liked to draw in school as a kid. Plus, I always liked to work with my hands, and I caught on pretty quickly. I found decorating pretty easy. I would take a toothpick and sketch out what I wanted to decorate on the cake and then draw it in with icing."

Since Dewey's was a family owned business, David's talents weren't just utilized in the icing department. He did everything from icing a cake and taking inventory on Sundays, to fixing the delivery trucks in the parking lot. "That's just the way it was in those days. It started to slow down the last couple of years, and I mainly iced cakes."

There are plenty of cakes and customers that stand out in David's mind. For example, for the 25th anniversary of Volkswagen, David was asked to make a car cake-- one that resembled Herbie. David was given several sheet cakes stacked together and a picture of the car. That was it. But David had his imagination and hands to follow his instincts. "I just started carving it out. I had an idea in my head and started cutting. Usually, I can envision what I want it to look like; so I just start cutting the cake into the shape that I need." The cake perfectly resembled a car.

Another group who always wanted a cake, was the Hell's Angels. "I've probably done about one hundred cakes for them. I would always make sure I did my best because you don't want to mess up a cake for that group." David chuckles and adds, "They were always very nice."

David relays another story that makes him laugh, "One customer I had would ask for a birthday cake for her husband each year. She never told him that I was making them," David smiles. "One day she called in a panic because her husband wanted to know how she iced the black tires on his tractor cake. I told her how but never heard from her again. I think her husband finally caught on."

Another tractor cake that David made for a customer brought tears to the man's eyes. "A girl brought a picture of her dad's old tractor. She called me the next day and said when he saw the cake he started crying and wouldn't let anybody eat it." David also recalls, "One woman told me I made her son's birthday cakes from the time he was born until the time he was in college."

When David decided to recently retire, a co-employee noted that "...with his departure, it is really is an end to an era..." It was also calculated how many cakes David had decorated-- about 416,000 cakes. The number of cakes he has made? Zero. David has never baked a single cake, only iced them. However, when asked what his favorite cake is, David answers without hesitation, "Strawberry cake with strawberry icing that my sister-in-law makes." As for the number of cakes he has decorated since he retired-- just one. I would have to say this is one neighbor who has a pretty sweet story.

Do your job 150%.

THE KEY TO YOUTH

A Spry Gal

Mary Lou Fitzgerald appears to be the age of someone who would use a walker or carry a cane. However, this spry gal is far from behaving old. When telling a story, Mary Lou's eyes widen and her eyebrows raise animatedly. Her zestful enthusiasm is contagious as she engages you with fun, historical facts. Like my grandmother, she is proud to tell you how things once were. And what a story she has to tell.

Mary Lou moved here from California in 1967 with her husband, Jim. Back then, Clemmons had one grocery store, one gas station, two restaurants, and one pharmacist. Jim was a successful race car driver whose race car partner was actor, Paul Newman. Mary Lou said that racing was her husband's baby and her daughter was hers. Initially, she stayed at home with her daughter. Then, one day, a job was offered to her in a most peculiar way.

"My poodle needed to be trained. We were told an orthopedic doctor could do it," Mary Lou says with a smile. She went to the doctor's office and sat with her dog in a waiting room full of adults who were there to be consulted about their orthopedic needs. When Mary Lou and the poodle were called in to meet the doctor, Mary Lou was asked if she worked. The doctor admitted she needed a medical assistant and would work around Mary Lou's schedule. With only a high school diploma, Mary Lou was trained to work in the operating room. But she was not just a medical assistant, Mary Lou tells me.

"Those were the days, Honey, where we didn't have computers. We did everything by hand. I did all the insurance and the billing, too." Mary Lou became the orthopedist's right hand woman and the best of friends. They went to medical seminars all over the world. "She took me to Europe, then, China, Egypt, Africa, and Switzerland. Luckily, my daughter was in high school, so I could travel some." After many years in the medical field, Mary Lou became an honorary member of Forsyth Stokes Davie Medical Assistance and honorary member of the North Carolina State Medical Assistance.

"Then I retired in 1985," Mary Lou says as she lets out a chuckle. "I sort of retired. I was asked to help open Triad Home Therapeutics." Mary Lou also became politically active in Clemmons. "I was asked to the be the campaign manager for Pat Sheptard (The first elected mayor in Clemmons.) And she won. But, the very next day, my husband was killed (during a race), and she and the whole campaign crew came over and helped out a lot." Actor Paul Newman also showed support and gave the eulogy at Holy Family Catholic Church in Clemmons.

Not one to linger on painful past events, Mary Lou changes the subject, "You know, I am the poster child for my doctor?" I find out Mary Lou is a three-time cancer survivor. She beat breast cancer twice and won a bout with lung cancer. At one point, she was told she only had five to six years to live. So, she flew to Ireland with her daughter despite being hairless from the treatment. "I was a little baldy," she laughs. I asked why she sought out the luck of the Irish. "It was maybe a little celebration of life."

She beat the cancer and the prediction of her life span. With all her battles, you would think Mary Lou would be physically strapped. But throughout our conversation she hops up from her chair like there's a springboard under her and shows me various pictures.

"You're very vivacious. What do you attribute this to?" I ask the lady whose energy I envy.

"I've always kept up with friends. And probably because I've traveled. I think you learn to appreciate meeting new people when you travel." With her lively spirit, it's no surprise that Mary Lou volunteers. For twenty years, she coordinated drivers in Clemmons for Meals On Wheels. For the last three years, she has worked for the Ronald McDonald Room at Forsyth Hospital. She also helps with the linens at the Holy Family Church and previously wrote the offertory, a task she enjoyed. "I loved that job. It kept my mind alert." With a smile she adds, "I'm just so lucky to be here. I've never met anyone that wasn't beautiful. I'm just so happy." And Clemmons is happy to have her.

"What do you like best about living here?" I ask our neighbor.

"I loved Clemmons at first because it was so small. I still love it, but it seems overwhelming. When we put that new hospital in, I thought, we are a big town now." Then Mary Lou looks as if she has an epiphany. "Maybe, I'll volunteer at that hospital... Yes. I will." And just like that, the spunky Mary Lou added one more item on her to-do list.

New experiences keep our minds young.

Neighborly, Noble, and Nice

He is a man who still uses the phrase, "...that will be fine and dandy." Mr. James Coghill always tries to give a high-five attached with a smile when passing a student in the halls of West Forsyth High School. The former teacher became an athletic trainer in 1986 and has been helping the school for over forty years now. It would seem life at West is like oxygen keeping the body alive for this spirited guy.

Proof of that may lie in the high tally of times being recognized. He has been called the "Ultimate Titan." In 2002, the *Cronus*, West Forsyth's yearbook was dedicated to Jim, noting his most popular beliefs of what kind of life one should lead. That is, to be, "Neighborly, noble, and nice." So where did this inspiring neighbor gets his admirable traits from? There are five people in particular who have had their influence.

"My wife," Jim says, "has definitely made me a better person. We have such a workable relationship. We have been able to kind of gel in one sense of the word. My wife is a very strong person. She has moved me in the right direction in our life and has always been supportive of my work at West."

In addition to the accolades he has for his wife, Kathy, Jim speaks about his parents. "My father was a very reserved gentleman, but very jovial and lively. He would be the epitome of neighborly, noble, and nice." Jim adds with a grin, "He loved saying, 'If you cant say anything nice don't say anything at all.'" Then, thinking about his mother, Jim mentions, "My mother spoke her mind. Mother died fourteen years ago. But she was aware of me being a very happy person doing what I love. I think they would be rather proud."

Two influential teachers in Jim's life were a high school history teacher and an English teacher. "My history teacher drove us to hear JFK speak in Chapel Hill. I thought, 'I want to do something like that.' And when I was teaching, we went to Raleigh and D.C." Jim remembers his English teacher who was always grammatically correct. "She had us remember poems-- poem A, poem B and everyone chose poem A to memorize. She said, 'I will give a nickel to someone who memorizes poem B. I said, 'I will.' I still have that nickel."

When pressed, Jim will share the effect he has had on his students in his years teaching and working in the school system. For instance, Jim has been in charge of looking over the kids who must serve in-school suspension. One girl rebelled against Jim and any other nearby authority. A couple of years ago, Jim saw her at the store. "She said to me, 'You had the most influence on me because you did not give up on me.' I think she didn't get her degree until she was thirty-two-years-old and is now a speech pathologist."

With a big heart and open mind, I ask the gentleman if there is anything folks may not know about him. He says he is proud of the fact his children graduated from West and that is he has two grandchildren. However, a fact unknown to others, he states, "I'll be seventy on November 3rd." The news comes as a surprise considering the youthful vitality he possesses. While he might be entering a new decade in his life, this neighbor is a walking example of the quote by George Burns, "You can't help getting older, but you don't have to get old."

The purity of children keep us vibrant.

Would you?

There is a man who is trying to "Pay It Forward" in Clemmons. The kind gesture is an idea that stems from the movie, *Pay It Forward.* Kevin Spacey, who plays a teacher in the movie, challenges his students to create a plan that will change the world. Hayley Joel Osment is one of Spacey's students and comes up with the concept to, "Pay It Forward." Hayley Joel Osment's plan involves repaying a good deed by doing something positive for three new people. The belief, then, is that those three people will do something good for others and so on.

Is Hayley Joel Osment here in Clemmons spreading the good karma? No, but Nick Jongebloed is. Each Sunday morning, Nick takes his dog, Sampson, to Tanglewood Park-- a treat for Sampson, since attention is usually shared with the foster dogs Nick has at home. After the two play ball at the park, they go to Starbucks. Nick orders a coffee with a side of whip cream for his dog. Once Nick gets to the drive-thru window, he pays for his coffee and for the person behind him. Nick got the idea three months ago from a friend on Facebook.

"I saw a friend who posted on Facebook that she was surprised that someone had paid for her coffee at Starbucks. I thought that was a great idea and I should start doing that," Nick says. He also believes his act is just good energy. "I'm a big believer in what goes around comes around. The people at Starbucks are always nice and Sampson appreciates the whip cream," Nick laughs as he gives his dog a pat on the head that results in a big wet lick from Sampson. "And it's

75

not like I'm buying anything expensive, it's just a cup of coffee."

When asked if karma has worked in his favor since he started, "paying it forward", Nick says, "I try to be positive, which is funny because I'm a Business Analyst and it's my job to study the downside to scenarios. So I always prepare myself for what I believe to be the worst case, but I anticipate things will work out well-- and typically they do. I think I'm just a very lucky person." Call it luck or call it karma, the small gesture seems to be contagious.

"Usually, when I leave the drive-thru and pay for the coffees, I'm just in a really good mood. Plus, the employees at Starbucks have said that sometimes they have others who will do the same and pay it forward, too."

If given the chance, would you pay it forward?

Walking the Walk

Who would know better about the benefits of walking than Neal and Joyce Johnson? Most elderly couples may wind down during their retired age, but not these two. Neal and Joyce walk four or five miles about five or six times a week. Their swift pace is noticeable. However, there is something else about this pair that catches one's eye. The cute couple holds hands as they walk.

"I think he holds my hand so that I can pull him up the hill," Joyce laughs.

"Yeah," Neal smiles, "I need to hold on to her."

"He let me fall once," Joyce jokes, referring to a time when she lost her footing. A trip here or there is bound to happen when

walking as long as the Johnson's have."We've been walking for..."
Joyce begins mentally tallying up the years. Then as couples do,
who have been together for forty five years like these two have,
Neal finishes her sentence.

"We've been walking forever," he says.

"I would say it's the last twenty years that we've really
been hitting it," Joyce continues.

"We try to walk everyday," Neal says.

"If it's cold or rainy, we walk at the Y," says Joyce.

"Outside, we walk mostly in our area, on Peacehaven or
near Lasater Lake." Neal adds.

"And we like to walk outside because there is more to see,"
Joyce says. "I will walk if it's cold, but I don't really like to go if
it's below sixty degrees."

But Neal will go unless it is "...below fifty. In the summer,
we go early in the morning."

"Or late in the morning," Joyce says with a flirty grin while
gazing at her husband.

Neal teases and says, "I can't get her out of bed."

Joyce laughs and adds, "I've earned it."

The two met in their home state of North Dakota. Joyce
raised their three boys while Neal worked as a pharmacist. Next,
they lived in Ohio for twenty years. The couple finally settled in
Clemmons in 1986. Nowadays, when the two are not walking, you
can find Joyce helping out with the grandchildren Monday through
Friday.

"I make sure they get off of the bus and do their homework
until their mother gets home. Sometimes, they will come to our
house for dinner." While Joyce lends a motherly hand with the

next generation, Neal enjoys volunteering at the Clemmons Masonic Lodge and the Winston-Salem Shrine Club.

Neal and Joyce also enjoy driving their motorhome. "I'm one of twelve siblings," Joyce says. "I'm number eleven. Eight out of the twelve have had motorhomes. We've been able to travel to all fifty states." Neal, who is the President of the Carolina Ramblers Motorhome Group and the National Director of the Family Motor Coach Association, talks about their next trip.

"In May, we are going out to Gillette, Illinois, for the Family Motor Coach Association's 50th celebration. We will go there, to Colorado, and back to North Dakota-- to see family," Neal says.

"He loves driving. He could drive all day," Joyce says.

"We try to drive 400 miles a day, usually. We've been blessed with good health and that's what has kept us going," Neal says.

Maybe their good health also has to do with their walking. Or maybe it is the healthy relationship the two have had for forty-five years. "She's adorable with people and has the best personality ever. She's a very loving and caring person," Neal says.

"Neal is very patient," Joyce explains. "He doesn't have an angry bone in his body." Seems as if these two neighbors were meant to go hand-in-hand in all walks of life.

Produce some endorphins. Exercise to feel vibrant.

The Dancer

When a student steps into Jacqui Chance's science classroom at Forsyth Country Day, they are not told to sit down. They are not told to open their books. Instead, Mrs. Chance turns on music and has everyone dance with Barney Bones-- the skeleton in the front of her classroom.

"If a child comes in after another class and you tell them to open their book again, they'll fall asleep," says Jacqui. "So I turn on some music and we move our cranium with Barney. We lift our clavicles up and down. We jump up and down on our femurs, patellas, and fibulas," says Jacqui with a great big grin as her eyes light up. "Afterwards, we can sit down with a more focused academic approach. But I make sure everything we do is hands-on. Kids need to manipulate and create."

With so much energy herself, I wonder who enjoys and needs to get up and dance more-- the kids or Jacqui-- or both. When prompted about her vivacity, Jacqui admits with a laugh, "I don't have as much energy as I once did." Jacqui, who is an Ohio native, grew up seeing her mom teach.

"My mom was a swimming teacher in the summer. As a young kid, I would tag along with her and help her," Jacqui giggles, "I thought I was helping her-- I was probably more of a pain. But as I got older, I taught swimming and dancing." Jacqui had been training as a dancer since she was little and could have made a professional living out of it, but felt her dancing days eventually would be numbered. Thus, she pursued a college degree in biology at Boston University. Jacqui then went to New York City where she attained her master's degree from Columbia University while also teaching physical education at the Greenwich Village Montessori school.

While teaching was her natural calling, Jacqui still honored her love for dance. In fact, she danced professionally in New York City while also teaching and attaining her master's. Thus, she began to incorporate her two passions into one. Jacqui began to examine the state curriculum and creative movement. And once Jacqui moved to North Carolina, she became a physical education teacher at FCD where she combined her love of teaching and dance.

After being a P.E. teacher for a while, Jacqui decided to use her biology background and become a science teacher for kindergarten through fourth grade. She also started, Summer Quest, which is a summer enrichment program. Jacqui can also be seen teaching a workshop at Salem College. "I teach a Methods Workshop on integrating different disciplines into your class, science, math, and movement." Dancing in her classrooms is not the only place you can find Jacqui. She also volunteers at the Clemmons Food Pantry once a month and is a Eucharistic Minister at Holy Family. "It's my vehicle for spiritual centering."

Jacqui says she feels really lucky to have met her "partner in crime," her husband, Larry. "We are best friends. We love hanging out whether it's traveling, hiking or biking-- we try to work as a team during good times and bad times," Jacqui says. "You know life is like a giant puzzle-- sometimes things don't quite fit and sometimes doors open. But whether it's going for a walk, or quietly working by yourself in the garden, you need that quiet time to synthesize and to create a paradigm to find a way to get through the roller coaster of life." Jacqui also adds, "I think having an open mind, faith-- and if you really work at something-- you can make a very happy and satisfying life. I get that through teaching and just seeing the sparkles in kids eyes when they experience a scientific experiment or the joy of dance and play."

No doubt, the zest and love of dance that our neighbor enjoys sharing with her students could bring out the best in almost any child. In fact, this neighbor seems to be the type who could bring out the inner child in anyone.

Snap your fingers. Shake your shoulders. You do not need dancing shoes, just a song to tap a beat and dance!

The Coffee Maker

Forty years. Forty years is how long Dean Matlock has been making coffee at Clemmons Moravian Church for the Lovefeasts. The Clemmons native has lived here since 1941 and was recently presented with a plaque from the church for his service. The plaque will appropriately hang in the coffee kitchen. The coffee kitchen was built two years ago to help service the Lovefeast ceremonies on Christmas Eve. A service Matlock first began because, "I always worked with my father. I worked at Taylors Brothers Tobacco. I worked with him on the farm and when he went to serve coffee, I just naturally went with him."

When young Dean followed his father in the church he found, "...a fairly big aluminum pot. We had a gas stove that would heat the water up. Mother would tie up a pound of coffee in a sack. And that's how we fixed fifty cups of coffee-- with a sack sitting in a huge pot of boiling water. We would get dippers to scoop the coffee out and pour it into tea kettles. We would then pour the coffee into the coffee cups to serve." Then, Dean would have to prepare for the next service-- which meant cleaning the old cups of coffee. Who cleaned each cup by hand while brewing more cups of coffee for the next service? That's right. Dean did. "It was pretty hectic," Dean recalls.

"But, later, the services got bigger and we had to buy bigger pots. At first we served an average of sixty-five cups per service. Now, we serve about three-hundred to four-hundred cups per service." With the new coffee kitchen, the brewing business has become a little easier. "We have a big stainless steal pot. The water goes on the outside then the pots go inside of that. There's also a filter inside of it," says Dean. "Then we push the brew button and let the hot water run through-- kind of like a coffee maker-- but I can make four-hundred cups now." As Dean describes the enormous coffee pot with the use of his hands as if he is brewing the coffee right there, he also confides about one very beneficial amenity. "We now have a dishwasher."

While grateful he does not have to wash cups by hand, Dean will also admit he always been good with his hands. He says, "I've always been mechanically minded." The trait came in handy in the tobacco business when fixing machines and building machines that helped pack tobacco into paper pouches.

However, the time it seemed extremely helpful was when Dean's dad was working on his 1936 Ford car. Dean's dad had taken the wheels off and put the car on cinder blocks. Somehow the car fell on top of Dean's dad. Neighbors were trying to lift the car up but it was too heavy. Quickly thinking on his feet, Dean put one of the blocks beside the car, put a long metal bar on top of it to use as a levy, and lifted the car up. He saved his dad. "I don't remember what Dad said after that, but I do remember his chest being real sore for a long time afterwards," Dean says rubbing his own chest. Dean, who always remained close with his dad, is close with his four children and nine grandchildren, too.

"We have one great grandchild and another will be coming soon," Dean says with a sense of pride. "Every Sunday, we all eat together and sit around at my house. My wife and I fix a meal and feed them all." Do they provide coffee? "Always. I drink mine straight black." Dean will continue to make coffee each Sunday for his family and for the Lovefeasts as well.

"I'm going to keep making it as long as my health is good and they'll keep letting me. In ten more years, it will be fifty years that I will be serving it." And who would not want to enjoy a nice cup of joe from a neighbor who makes it with so much warmth from his heart?

If you serve others for a long time, they eventually look up to you.

The Farmer

Sweet potatoes, peppers, squash, tomatoes, broccoli, lima beans, cantaloupe, and watermelon are just some of the plants that Frank Wilkins grows in his garden. How does he decide what to grow? In his mind, it is simple.

"People tell me what they want," Frank simply says in a deep voice. While one would argue that Frank certainly qualifies as a farmer with his three tractors and vast array of plants springing up from Clemmons' clay soil, Frank states, "I'm not a farmer. I'm retired. But I've had a garden everywhere I have lived."

The local restaurants who receive free produce from Frank would beg to differ that he is retired. Plus, with how busy the the garden keeps him, Frank seems to almost work longer hours than what his typical workday was as a teacher. He taught woodworking for seventeen years. But like an interested student, Frank likes to constantly learn about gardening and how he might improve.

"Every year, I learn something new. Last year, I had huge cauliflower heads, but they weren't white. They were green. I found out that you are supposed to put a rubber band around the leaves to help protect the cauliflower from the sun," Frank humbly remarks. "People will ask me questions, but I don't have all the answers. There is always room for improvement."

Something else Frank has picked up along the way to better gardening is, "A tablespoon of salt to a gallon of water prevents the moths from getting on the broccoli." It is solutions like these that help Frank keep his plants as organic as possible. "I put mulch around the plant. It keeps the sun from baking the soil. I also use fish emulsion which organically helps tomato plants. Two tablespoons of fish emulsion every two weeks-- if you feed them and nourish them, they will grow." Frank is also smart about using his resources. "Every year, I go to the Village of Clemmons and they give me as many dump trucks full of leaves as I want. I put them all over the yard and I put lime on it, which decomposes the soil."

Farming is not the only way this Vietnam War veteran passes his time. Frank also makes furniture, a craft demonstrated throughout his house and in his woodshop which he built beside his garden. Regarding one piece of furniture built from scratch,

Frank says, "I got the wood out of an old Cotton Mill in Virginia. It is rich, yellow, pine, and it is beautiful."

Aside from his adept ability with a hammer and saw, Frank also plays competitive table tennis three times a week. Frank says he has long enjoyed athletic endeavors, including the chance to excel in springboard diving. "I went to Stanton Military Academy for springboard diving. Then I went to a French-speaking school for one year in Switzerland for skiing." He was not only involved in gymnastics, he also coached it for years while teaching. In fact, Frank was the one who first opened Clemmons Gymnastics. He sold it five years ago. "I've been very fortunate and very blessed. My dad was a surgeon and when he retired he was very unhappy because he didn't know what to do with his time. I stay very busy."

Staying busy means keeping his garden growing-- including big Halloween pumpkins. "This is my first year growing pumpkins. I'll probably just give them away to somebody," Frank says. "Like I said, I'm very blessed." In light of all of the E. coli and Salmonella outbreaks that have plagued some of the more popular national brands in the last couple of years, it may be all of us who should be grateful for our neighbor's loving attention to his crops that he so freely shares with our community.

Find a hobby that makes you grow.

The Friend

He's just that type of person. The type that you talk to for five minutes and feel like you have known forever. Gene Livengood is a personable kind of guy who will meet someone once and turn around and invite him over for dinner. Why? "It's just in my nature," Gene says with a shrug of the shoulders. "It's easy for me to meet people and I don't know if it's my beard or what, but a lot of people will say, 'Hey Gene' and I won't know them, but I say 'Hi' back."

Maybe it is the thick dark beard that blankets Gene's face. Or maybe it is because Gene has lived in Clemmons since 1950 and is one of the longest-living residents in the area. "I was raised poor with holes in the bottom of my shoes and patches on my overalls. As kids we didn't know better. When I got older, I began to realize that others had more money. But for me, people are people. My philosophy is if you get to know more people, you know more about who you are dealing with."

After living in Clemmons for so long, Gene has certainly come in contact with a lot of people. Gene recalls the Clemmons he grew up in. "Lewisville-Clemmons Road was just two lanes. There was a farm instead of the Pizza Hut and a field of hay where Wendy's is now located. Old Meadowbrook neighborhood was owned by Mr. Lasater. It was a huge farm. I know the first house that was built in Old Meadowbrook and who lived there," says Gene. "Clemmons West neighborhood was a dairy farm. But as the older folks moved out, the younger folks would sell off the land because they weren't going to farm." Gene did not become a farmer either. He first worked at the Shell Gas Station as a Service Station Attendant.

"We would fill cars up with gas and wash and clean them, too." Gene said he met a lot of people working there. But it was at RJR that he earned a living for over thirty years. "I started out as what is known as a 'day laborer' but worked the night shift. I eventually advanced to look after two crews overhauling machinery from one factory to another." Gene also got involved with coaching sports. He began coaching at Southwest Little League for some of the boys teams.

"I love to work with children. It's very rewarding for me." Then, his daughter began to play. "My daughter was the first girl to play Little League with the boys. When they started doing softball for the girls, I started coaching the girls. I got to know a lot of parents that way."

Gene coached softball and baseball for about ten years. He also coached football. Known as the Clemmons Broncos now, Gene says the football team was known as the Clemmons Cowboys back then. "I tried to work with kids who didn't have as much ability and teach them you can be a part of the group. I still get a lot of joy out of it when youngsters come up and talk to me." In fact, Gene still talks to those who he coached. "One of my neighbor's went to Clemmons High School with me, and I coached my other neighbor in football." Since his coaching days are done, Gene finds other ways to occupy his time.

"I do have the patience to sit three or four hours to hunt," says Gene. "I do love watching sports-- just about any sport and any team. But really, it's so relaxing for me just to get out on that John Deere and mow the lawn. There are no distractions, no phone calls... and I do love a good yard."

Maybe it is because of his relaxing activities that Gene has such a good spirit. Or maybe it is just like he said-- in his nature. "If people know Gene, they know Gene. I'm a man of my word, we don't have to have a contract on that. If I tell you something, I would like to think you could take me to the bank. I'm just that type of person. I just want to be accepted and accept other people. I want to be as real as I possibly can."

Hearing how Gene used to work at a gas station (when they still called them service stations), makes me wistful for the good old days. Knowing that there are people like Gene who do not need to put their intentions in writing so that you can count on them, make me grateful there are still neighbors like that to be found in Clemmons. It is nice to still be able to take a neighbor at his word.

Make an effort to be a good friend and they will be a good friend to you.

The Resident Angel

When arriving in the emergency room, you are told to wait. You are told to be patient. It seems as if no one is ever going to take care of you. But if your lucky, you will be greeted by a petite, compassionate elderly woman named, Lee Smith. She is the kind of person who can relieve some of your anxiety with her kind bright eyes and patient tone of voice. Lee, a resident of Clemmons for forty-one years, has helped folks through her volunteer work at both Forsyth Medical Emergency Room and in the nursery at Baptist Hospital for almost twenty-five years.

When asked about her exceptional length of service, she bashfully says, "I don't feel like I am special by any means, I do it because I love people and I love being around people." It is easy to see Lee finds her job very rewarding when she tells this story, "One lady who I helped wrote a letter and said I was her angel. I remember that because I've never been called an angel before. I just try to treat people how I would like to be treated when a loved one is facing a serious illness."

As a volunteer, Lee helps greet patients, takes them to triage, or escorts visitors back to see those who are ill. "I try to smile, I try to treat every visitor and patient as though they are special. People who come in to the ER are stressed, upset, and sometimes they are not at their best. I try to put myself in their shoes and see how they feel and try to overlook any pushiness."

For her hard work at Forsyth, Lee was inducted into the Lifetime Organization in 2009, which is almost like an Honor Society for volunteers. At Baptist Hospital, Lee earned "Volunteer of the Year" in 1997 and "Volunteer of the Month" in 2007.

"I told Baptist hospital, I would almost pay you to let me come and feed these babies because they are such a joy." As a mother myself, it is nice to know there are people like Lee caring for our babies like a mother would.

The volunteer work for this spry lady does not stop in the medical field. At Clemmons Moravian Church, Lee serves as the secretary for the "Young At Heart Senior Friends" and is a representative for their Advisory Board. She also helps the church's nursery and is active in the Women's Fellowship group. Plus, Lee has served buns and coffee for over fifty years as a Diener at the Lovefeast.

Her true love, was her husband, Bill. They were married for almost fifty four years before he died. What a love story. When asked how she handled his passing, she answered, "I had to pray a lot about being alone because Bill and I were best friends." Lee began volunteering again a month after he passed. "There must be a reason God kept me here. I think Bill would be proud of me for going on," Lee says.

So why does this humble Clemmons resident give so much of her time and energy to others?

"I don't do it for the praise, I do it because it makes me feel like a worthwhile individual. I try to give back for the good life that I have had."

I would say Clemmons is lucky to have such a caring member in its community. It might not even be a stretch to consider that we have our own resident angel.

Become your own resident angel.

The Postwoman

As I head to the Post Office to mail a package to my sister in Washington, D.C., I get a smile on my face. As my package is being weighed and measured, I know I'm likely to be peppered with friendly inquiries about my family or my life in general. This trip is no exception.

"How is your son? I just love seeing how your family has grown up. Your brother has become such a gentleman," observes Cindy Doub, a veteran of the Clemmons Post Office of over eighteen years. It takes me over a minute to ask Cindy about her family because she always seems genuinely interested to hear about mine.

After a few minutes, I'm able to sneak in, "How are your grandkids?" Cindy's eyes light up. She has raised three kids to enjoy productive adulthoods, is grandmother to two gregarious grandkids and is happily anticipating the arrival of another one soon. Cindy marvels at the wonders of her role as Grandma.

"They love you unconditionally and you know what to expect. You don't worry about the little things as much."

During Cindy's tenure at the Clemmons Post Office, she has gotten to know most families in the area. What many patrons may be surprised to know is that Cindy's earlier career track included serving in the armed services. She joined the military in college as many young adults do in order to afford their education. Cindy was stationed in Hawaii as a mail clerk in the United States Army. She was also a mechanic.

Cindy eventually made her way to North Carolina because her husband hailed from this great state. Her postal service career began just one town over in Lewisville. She worked at the Lewisville Post Office for seven years and still keeps in touch with their retired postmaster, Della Mae Franklin, who is now in her mid-eighties. No surprise to anyone who knows and has spent time with Cindy.

It was this exact thought that got me thinking, "Cindy, just how many customers do you think you know?" I ask.

"We get a mix of people since we are on the border of Forsyth and Davidson counties. We think we know about 98%. I know that sounds high, but we don't have that many people that just come in and pass by. We have so many businesses in the area that their employees know they can come in to get what they need. The customers who have post office boxes will come in and say hello. We are glad to say hello back."

I probed her for a specific story about a customer that made an impression on her and Cindy instantly grins. "Recently, a lady came in and we asked her how her father was doing. She said that he had just gotten his license renewed and will be able to drive until he turns one-hundred and one years old." Can you imagine? "Although, the best part is the children. They really look forward to the lollipops, but seeing them grow up and the people they become -- it's wonderful."

Curious about the downfall to her profession, I ask Cindy what is the most challenging part of her day. "I love seeing the older generation. They're the ones who still write the letters, the thank you cards, and the birthday cards. They are not going to send a text message to someone." Cindy continues, "When they stop coming in, you know it's because they passed away, and that's hard." When asked what she likes best about working in Clemmons, Cindy answers, "Everybody works well together and helps each other out. I am grateful to work for the Post Office because it has provided a living for me."

Whether Cindy is dispensing stamps or helping her patrons fill out postal forms, she seems always ready to give personal attention and glad to exchange a quick story or family photo. She does so because she enjoys knowing that each neighbor and their family is doing well. What a wonderful way to put a stamp on our community.

Put your positive stamp on your community.

FAMILY SECRETS

A Gift

Rebecca Howorka has something in common with
Aristotle, Faith Hill, and Dave Thomas, the founder of Wendy's.
They were all adopted.

"The reason my parents adopted me is because there had
not been a girl born into the family in sixty-seven years," Rebecca
says. Eventually as she grew into adulthood, Rebecca became
more curious about her birth parents. At twenty-four years old,
Rebecca asked her adoptive father to do a search for her birth
parents. He was able to find them. Rebecca then flew to meet her
birth parents who eagerly awaited her arrival at the airport.

"My flight was delayed. I was supposed to get in at 8:00
p.m. but did not get in until 2:00 a.m. They sat there the whole
time waiting for me," Rebecca says.

As she began to get to know her birth parents, Rebecca was
able to piece together parts of her unfinished life puzzle. For
instance, Rebecca learned that her birth mom got pregnant at
eighteen and told no one about it except for Rebecca's birth father.
She delivered the baby alone in a different town and never told a

soul. Ten years later, Rebecca's birth parents had two more children.

"I have a blood brother and blood sister who are great." Rebecca adds, "I definitely look like my birth mother's family. Personality-wise, I'm a good mix of both of them." All the families mixed into this one melting pot feel lucky to have each other. "I would honestly have to say adoption hasn't affected me because of the love I have from my family and the security they have given me. I have more people that I can love and more people that can love me-- unconditionally." Rebecca reflects about what her adopted mother said about the experience, "'You can never have too many people love you.' My mother was very unselfish."

Being generous is a trait that must have been passed on to Rebecca. Two years ago, Rebecca's aunt, who is a diabetic, was on dialysis and needed a kidney. Who do you think stepped up to the plate?

"I never had surgery before, but my aunt needed a kidney. Plus, if she got a kidney and came home, then Uncle Ken got to leave the nursing home and come home, too." Rebecca recalls the surgery, "They fill you up with gases; and getting those gases out can be tiring and makes you feel crampy. I mean, they took an organ out so it's going to be painful. But overall, it worked out well. My aunt and I had zero complications after our recovery."

It is because of family nearby, that Rebecca and her husband decided to open an Express Oil and Auto Repair Shop in North Carolina. They left the corporate world to open a franchise that could withstand the economy lows but one that would also reflect their core values-- being honest, ethical, friendly and professional. With the money they have made, they have donated to Operation Blessing which distributes food to those in need.

They also financially donate to the Watch. It is a program in Murray, Kentucky, that helps adults with special needs. "What's cool is people bring jobs to these special needs adults. So if they need someone to screw on a bolt, these adults will do the job and get paid for each bolt that is screwed into place. No matter how small the task, these adults are glad to get it done."

Getting a job done is something that seems pretty natural to Rebecca, no matter what that might entail-- being a loving daughter, donating a kidney, running a successful business. It seems fitting, too, that this neighbor has more than one set of parents to be proud of her and all the fine ways in which she contributed to her family and community.

Give and you shall receive.

Motherly Instincts

Before knowing the truth behind his actions, Brenda Grabowski was told that her son, Nicholas "...was out of control.. that my child was a brat and needed to be reprimanded." Brenda says "Those comments are one of those things that you want to forget but, you never will."

As a mother, Brenda felt stung by outsider comments. She was also fearful inside her heart about what was really wrong with her son. She noticed at three years old, Nicholas showed signs of delayed speech. While searching for answers, Brenda felt blind. It was as if she was looking for a door in a dark room and only felt empty walls with her bare hands. She did not know the right questions to ask the doctors. The teachers at school could not help either.

"At preschool, when he was four, all we knew was that Nicholas couldn't stay on task. He needed a lot of one-on-one attention because he got distracted easily. He also liked being off by himself," says Brenda. Maybe he had Attention Deficit Hyperactivity Disorder, Brenda thought. But, that was not it. Finally, after having no clarity on the situation for months on end, the clouds dissipated. "After talking to the doctor and talking to the teachers, he was finally diagnosed. Nicholas is autistic." Brenda explains why the diagnosis was not immediately evident.

"Nicholas doesn't have the hand flapping like most autistic kids. He makes eye contact. His ability to understand and comprehend what others are saying is difficult. So people don't always know that he is autistic." Brenda says she has had to really work with the teachers and ask for a lot of help.

"I really feel that the school system in Forsyth County needs to be more educated in this area because the number of children who have autism is one in eighty-eight. It used to be one in one-hundred-fifty. In Nicholas's class, there are two kids who have it," says Brenda.

While there are challenges for an autistic child in the classroom, Brenda has also discovered how incredibly intelligent Nicholas is compared to his peers. "He knew all of his kindergarten words in the first week of school; so now they are challenging him and he's working on first grade words. He's also reading at a first grade level."

Brenda says she has never been one to ask for help, but with all of her family in Michigan, Brenda learned to lean on others. "The people who have helped me have become my family. Everyday can be a struggle, but I can say that all the other moms and personal educators I have met have been phenomenal." Brenda

says she has also found support by having "...a good pediatrician."
She believes it is also important for other parents to act if you think
something is wrong with your child. If you are looking for
something more in depth, "I would go to a behavioral pediatrician,
a developmental pediatrician or a neuropsychologist."

Then, with tears in her eyes, Brenda's devotion is evident
when she says, "It's been a rough year. He's made so much
progress but its been a challenge at times. I think the toughest part
for any parent is wanting them to succeed."

It is at this point of our interview, Nicholas walks up to his
mother without hesitation and wipes away her tears. He has not
spoken to me and still does not. His heart is fixated on one task--
parenting his parent.

"You're sad," Nicholas says as he sweeps another tear drop
off of his mother's wet cheek.

"Yes, but I love you, Buddy," Brenda says as she scoops
her son into her arms. Brenda does not tell Nicholas to run along
and play because of a conversation with another adult. The mother
stops her world to tend to her son. She gives him another squeeze.
"I love you, Buddy."

As Nicholas gets down, Brenda's red-stained eyes look in
mine. She says with a forced smile, "He's a fun-loving little guy.
And he loves his little brother. He can't get enough of him."
Brenda also adds with one more tear, "His brother is three and his
speech is delayed just like Nicholas's."

Brenda reaches for tender words, "Not every child is cookie
cutter. Every child is like a snowflake. They are all different.
Nicholas is a snowflake and while all his branches may not be
formed right now, they will form eventually."

This neighbor's warmhearted actions speak volumes of the type of character she possesses and will likely pass on to her sons. Her actions liken to a quote by Vera M. Kelly, "Snowflakes are one of nature's most fragile things, but just look what they do when they stick together."

Trust your instincts-- especially those motherly ones.

The Penner Pack

No pictures are hanging on the walls. The furniture is gone. The counters in the kitchen are bare. The Penner house might be desolate except for the hustling and bustling of all seven children. While it looks like someone may have played a disappearing trick with the household items, the reason the house is empty is because the Penners are about to move to Uganda for two years. All they can take are two suitcases and their carry-ons. It might seem unusual to hear about a family from Clemmons to pick up and move to Uganda. It is not so strange for Keith and Jena Penner. They have four biological children and three adopted Ugandan children-- all varying from the ages of six to seventeen.

"A lot of people assume since we are going to Africa, we will living in a village in a stick hut," Jena laughs.

Keith smiles and says, "We will have power and water and live in Kampala, where over two million people live. A lot of people are worried about our safety, but Ugandans are very friendly."

Ironically, Uganda was one place from which Jena did not want to adopt children. "Our goal was to adopt older kids with special needs," Jena says. "We had a child with Autism and one with Epilepsy, which neither are treated for anymore. But sometimes, when you parent kids with extra fun stuff like that, you feel you have the capacity to do it with another child. Africa was the one country I didn't want to adopt from because it is a war-torn country, and I was worried about handling emotionally torn kids. It was just a fear."

After a mission trip to Uganda in 2008, they "...developed a love for Uganda," says Keith.

The Penners have not only provided a home for orphaned children, they have also discovered the need for anesthesia providers in Ugandan communities. Surgeries, such as hernia repairs, appendectomies, or amputations are typically postponed for six months. Mothers who need c-sections are not operated on. As result, further complications develop that are all preventable. As a nurse anesthetist, Keith was able to put his skills to work in the medical field during their mission trips.

After realizing they could help more Ugandans, Jena and Keith decided to move to Uganda once the kids were out of the house-- or so they thought. "It became pretty obvious God wanted us there now," says Keith, who took a job at a hospital in Uganda which will pay him $300 a month.

Jena adds, "We felt like waiting for retirement was the easy way. Sometimes the easy way isn't what your called to do."

But what about the kids? How did they handle the news of moving to another country? "We needed everyone on board or we wouldn't do it," says Jena. "I think it will be helpful for our Uganda kids to see what their country is like. As for the others, our last biological child is so excited. The next one up, who is thirteen, is very excited. He's looking at it as an opportunity to finish high school early via homeschool. Our fifteen-year-old feels like he already has this built-in friends network. All of our kids have a lot of Uganda friends from our trips and have been able to keep in touch through Facebook." Jena mentions that her eldest son, who is a seventeen-year-old student at West, has probably had the the hardest time, but decided he wanted to go. Maybe that's because the entire Penner family seems to be very close.

But with a family of nine, how can that be? How does Jena and Keith do it all? "A lot of people assume our older kids take care of the younger kids. They don't. We chose to have kids and I don't think our older kids should have to take care of the others. Luckily, they are all sweet to each other," says Jena. "But each night at 7:30, we tell them good night and we love you-- now scat," she laughs. "It's because we know it's important to have 'us' time." Jena continues, "We always eat dinner together and have that family time everyday. I'm ok with setting a routine and sticking with it. I think in a large family, you have to." Something else Jena has been very disciplined about is losing weight, through a program called, "Grace and Strength Diet." Jena would send daily text messages to her assigned coach and conduct a video chat with some other ladies in the program. "I used to use food to celebrate. But I was able to retrain my brain and I don't crave sugar anymore." Her hard work paid off. Jena lost 103 pounds.

100 pounds is equivalent to the maximum allowable weight for the two suitcases each Penner family member will be able to take on their international flight to Uganda. While the Clemmons community will miss these nine neighbors, may the Penner pack have safe travels and a wonderful time as they meet their new African neighbors. Bon voyage!

Family comes first.

Mary the Mother & Donna the Daughter

They look similar. They act similar. In fact, they were even wearing identical shiny pink shoes the day I talked to them. The reason for the common traits and tastes they share, likely stems from the fact that Mary Bingham and Donna Merriman are mother and daughter. So when Donna, the daughter, decided to open up her own clothing store, it was only natural that her mother, Mary, would be her partner. When the two tell the story about how Fraleigh's Boutique all began, it becomes very clear how well their personalities play off of each other.

"I was working for a factory and they were closing. I didn't have a job," Donna began. "Daddy said, 'Why don't you open up a clothing store?'"

"Daddy said you should open the store or mommy said?" Mary corrects her daughter, as mothers do.

"Maybe it was mother," Donna smiles. "I don't know. But anyway, mother was trying to find a partner for me. She said I needed a good partner, and I said, 'What about you? What better partner than my best friend?'" Donna looks in her mothers direction and continues, "I had worked in other clothing stores during high school, so I did have some background in this industry. Mother had worked as a secretary before being a stay-at-home mom."

"Secretary? I wasn't a secretary," Mary says setting her daughter straight.

"You worked in an office. Didn't you type?" Donna asks.

Looking at me, Mary says, "I worked at Western Electric and typed. I taught myself to type. I became a fast typer and that's why they hired me. You see, I was sixteen. They wanted me to be eighteen and so I kind of lied and told them I was eighteen. They asked to see my birth certificate. But they hired me anyway. Then I became a mother and worked twenty-four/seven, three-hundred-sixty-five days a year. Because we didn't hire babysitters back then." Donna shakes her head yes in agreement and then proudly adds how their employees have been like family, too.

"Each member of the staff has worked here for twelve years or longer," Donna says with a grin. "We just retired two people after twenty-five years of service." She also explains the name of the store. "Mother's middle name is Francis. Mine is Leigh. We combined them together to name our store, Fraleigh's."

I then ask Donna a personal question, "What has been the worst and best part about working with your mom?"

"It's like this, Jill. We have vendors who pull up in campers and sell clothes to us at the store. I will go out to the camper and take a look at the clothes and pick items out while mother watches the store. Then she'll pick items out while I watch the store. Nine times out of ten we pick out the exact same products. It's really weird how close we are. It's really great to work with your mom everyday, your best friend. If you love what you do, you don't feel like you are coming into work everyday."

I ask Mary the same, "What's been the best and worst part about working with your daughter?"

"I don't know any worst. The best is because you are best friends. It was like an adventure starting up Fraleigh's because that's a big undertaking that you don't even dare dream about. But Honey, if we go out and buy clothes, we buy the same colors, the same sizes-- almost close to eighty percent of the time. I would say we are a lot of like. Donna is very patient and I am very impatient, so I would say that is our biggest difference."

While Mary is talking to me, her eyes turn to her daughter as she says, "If we go out to dinner, I'll pick Donna up and we will have worn the same identical sweater." The two giggle.

Donna adds, "So we try not to buy too much of the same things anymore because that seems to happen, often."

For the mother and daughter who seem more like gabbing girlfriends, I would say that starting up Fraleigh's has paid off for them. Not only because these neighbors have stayed in business through the good and bad economic times, but because they have been able to do what few family members can say-- spent everyday together for the last thirty years.

Cherish the times with your family and giggle like girlfriends.

The Sportscaster

A man, whose face was hidden behind his baseball cap, carried his two-year-old daughter as they petted horses at Tanglewood's stables one morning. The fresh smell of hay filled the air. During the work-week, one might usually see horseback riders, walkers, or other mothers-- very few fathers.

"Are you a stay-at-home dad?" I asked while holding my son and giving in to my curiosity.

"I work in the evenings," he replied.

"What do you do?" I asked.

Revealing his face, Kenny Beck said, "I'm the Sports Director for WXII."

After talking further, Kenny explained that when he was younger he dreamed of being the voice of a major league baseball team. However, while playing baseball in college, another opportunity was tossed into Kenny's corner. Instead of being the voice for a major league team, he was drafted to pitch for one. It was the Montreal Expos, now known as the Washington Nationals.

"I went to a tryout for the novelty of it and because my friend said I should come. I didn't expect anything, but was drafted on the 48th round on the last day of the draft. It was fun, but I don't miss the rigors of that lifestyle." Thus, Kenny traded in his baseball glove for broadcasting.

"I worked for the ABC station in Salisbury, Maryland," Kenny says. "While there, I was asked to be the best man at a wedding in North Carolina." After his trip, Kenny came back and told his wife how much he liked North Carolina. Then, Kenny applied for a reporting job at WXII. He was hired. Kenny and his wife, Amanda, left their native state of Maryland to head south.

At WXII, Kenny worked as a reporter and a weekend anchor for three years. But then he was offered an opportunity that seemed like a home run-- the Sports Director position. He did, however, pause for a moment to consider the way it may affect his personal life.

"When they presented me the opportunity to do sports, I first had to think about how this was going to effect my home life and how much it would affect my child because my wife was six months pregnant at the time. We talked about it and found a way to make it work." So how did they make it work?

"Thankfully my wife works from home. There are mornings when I have Carly and there are mornings when she goes to daycare. There are mornings when we are all together as a family. My wife's employer has been great and WXII has been very accommodating with our family," Kenny says.

Being a big family man, Kenny says there are advantages to this schedule. "I have been able to spend many mornings with Carly, and now Owen, that a lot of traditional working fathers may not get to do. I have been able to go to events or see some really cute things. So that time in the morning is precious." Kenny adds that there are still times he feels like he is missing out.

"I'm at home for maybe two dinners a week. I don't get to do story-time at night. But it's cool to hear that Carly sees me on TV and says, 'Daddy, Daddy.' Although she says that when she sees the main anchor," Kenny jokes. He also notes that because of his work schedule, he likes to spend all of his down time with family.

"We made a choice to give up a lot for our kids. We don't ever go out. It's not to say one way is right and one way isn't. It's just what we do. Everyday is an adjustment, but a wonderful kind of adjustment." Kenny wonders if one day, when Carly and baby Owen are teenagers (the time when Mom and Dad aren't fun to be around anymore) maybe he will do a story about one of his kids. "It would be a unique opportunity to cover them whether they are fans in the stands or out on the field."

While that is a fun idea for the future, Kenny's reality today is staying up late for the evening broadcasts and waking up early to change diapers. Yet, Kenny has had no problem taking one for his home team. It seems clear this neighbor, who covers our local sports stories, is the type of Dad who is always ready and willing to step up to the plate.

Be an involved Dad.

Finding Time

Some may recognize Sandra Mock as a co-worker at Wells Fargo. Many residents probably know Sandra by her position held on Lewisville's City Town Council. Serving as the town's Mayor Pro Tempore, Sandra received the most votes in this past election.

"I'm involved because I want to have a voice for the citizens. It's part of a way of giving back to the community. I've always been involved in some form of community service-- Boy Scouts, Girl Scouts and various roles in church." It's no surprise Sandra has been involved with affiliations such as the Boys and Girls Scouts, since she has two grown children. Others may be interested to learn that she adopted a child from China. How did that come about?

"Part of it was I went through a divorce and remarried the guy I dated my senior year of high school. He had no children. I always wanted more children. We looked at national and international adoption and we chose to go internationally." Sandra has also served as a foster parent to several children in crisis. "Having foster kids is a way to have grandkids without having grandkids," Sandra laughs. In seriousness she adds, "It's a very challenging yet very rewarding opportunity. Children come from all walks of life. All situations are different, but it's the little strides they make everyday, the improvements, the more open they become and the warmth they show that makes the challenges worth it all."

Sandra says her three children are her greatest accomplishments in life. Then Sandra shows me a text she sent to her son that reads, 'If I ever get dementia like my mama, I just want you to know that I love you. Even if I can't tell you, just remember that I'll always love you." Something else Sandra is proud of is the fact that she has instilled in her children the importance of giving back to others. "My twenty-nine year old son is a foster parent and my twenty-year old daughter is a certified nursing assistant at a nursing facility while she also attends school full-time."

With Sandra's full-time schedule that includes parenting, working at Wells Fargo, and volunteering for the community, the only time she can exercise is at 5:30 a.m. She meets a group of walkers at the town plaza. "I have to work out early or I would never do it at all." I ask Sandra how she does indeed do it all. "Schedules," Sandra says insistently as if she has answered the question before. "It's all about schedules. I have had to adjust my schedule at Wells Fargo. It's also called having a great husband, great friends, and children who are flexible. My husband and I look to see where things can fit in the schedule. My friends will help pick my daughter up sometimes. Having great friends who don't mind helping out and having a great support group makes a difference, too."

Sandra looks lovingly at her daughter, Olivia, who has sat patiently throughout the interview. "You find time to make what's most important to you work. I'm not one who sit downs and reads or watches a lot of TV. I would rather be doing something." I ask Sandra if there is something few people know about her. "I like auctions, flea markets, and antiques. But, I'm pretty much an open book." Most public servants do have to be an open book when representing their citizens. This neighbor adds one chapter in our collective community book that makes for inspirational reading.

Turn off the TV and do something.

REACHING DESTINATIONS

The Judge

One of our neighbors has been described as Forsyth's judicial champion. In fact, he holds the highest position on the district court bench. In the seven elections that he has run as Chief District Court Judge, he has only been opposed twice. The neighbor I am referring to is Honorable Judge William Reingold. He has a list of achievements that is long and respectable.

However, Judge Reingold believes his life could have taken another path and it would have been him being judged, "It could have been me on the other side of the bench." Coming from a family in which no one went to college, Judge Reingold explains, "Intuitively, I think I knew education was the only way to get ahead."

While Judge Reingold did not know any lawyers growing up, much less judges, his job as a tennis pro after college introduced him to some. "They spurred my interest. I wanted to get a job that could make a difference in someone's life but there was also a good chance I could make a good living as well. I thought it was a win-win situation." Thus, Judge Reingold applied to various law schools and set his sites on Wake Forrest University.

After graduating as a Demon Deacon, Judge Reingold served as a prosecutor. "Don Tisdale was the District Attorney and hired me to be a prosecutor for $17,000 a year. I thought I had died and gone to heaven," Judge Reingold chuckles as he thinks about the small salary. But soon he would be making much more due to his dedicated work ethic. Judge Reingold become appointed to judge after only two and an half years of being a lawyer. Then, in 1998, he was appointed as Chief District Court Judge and has since served in that position. Not one to rest on his proverbial laurels, he has worked to make his time on the bench meaningful.

"The Chief District Court Judge has the authority to create courts. I wanted to take our courts in a direction they had not been before," says the Judge. He explains he was not satisfied with simply deciding whether or not there was sufficient reason to put a person behind bars. Rather, he wanted to work towards alleviating problems and finding solutions that would help people avoid the courtroom again.

"We created a juvenile drug court, a domestic drug court, a truancy court and a mental health court. We have also modified some other courts, increasing how much time we devote to child support collection. I thought it was important to treat families as a whole instead of addressing just one member," Judge Reingold explains. "For example, if you have one kid strung out on drugs and he gets clean but goes back to the same environment, it's a very good chance the same thing will happen again. I, along with my colleagues, agreed we wanted to get the entire family involved." It is the cases about family and the custody of children that the Judge says can keep him up at night.

"It's easy to lose sleep over custody cases because you are affecting the life of a child. You make the best decision you can, but often times, you see two very good people and you know you have to break someone's heart." Perhaps, one of the reasons these types of cases are difficult for Judge Reingold is because of the closeness he shares with his own two sons.

"My proudest achievements are framed up on the wall," he says referring to the pictures of his eighteen and twenty-year old sons. As a father who is clearly interested in the well-being of his children, he makes sure his sons are a priority even during strenuous workdays. "When you are exhausted and your son needs you, you just do it. You prioritize what's important to you."

While his sons are off to college, they will likely appreciate his sage advice and fatherly help for years to come. On the subject of retiring from the bench, the Judge says there are still certain programs to which he would like to devote his time.

"I'm in my twenty-seventh year and I'm a lot closer to retiring, but there are a few things I want to finish. One thing I am working on is the program, 'Reclaiming Futures.' The biggest thing they do that I like is every child that now comes in the legal system must get screened for substance abuse issues and mental health issues. There's also a mentor program that comes from that. The beauty of that is Wake Forest Law School has stepped up and is providing mentors."

In terms of mentors, it seems this neighbor has served as one to our community as well. What Judge Reingold knew intuitively, before he ever earned a single college credit, he used to build an admirable career. He then made sure to use his education and experience to help members of our community have the same opportunities.

Your past does not create your destiny, you do.

The Southern Belle

Because my husband is from Nebraska and I am from North Carolina, we always compare the south and the midwest. Even though I was born in the midwest and have family in Illinois, I grew up in the south. I am accustomed to the sizzling summers, mild winters and of course-- southern charm. My husband will occasionally point our state's characteristics, although I think he has become almost thoroughly immersed into our southern melting pot himself.

Someone else who is getting a taste of the southern life is Katie Sheldon. Katie is petite in stature with a big heart. She moved from Ohio to Clemmons about six months ago. Her husband, Brad, was hired at B.E. Aerospace. The mother of fifteen-month-old, Brooklynn, has made a new home for her family in Clemmons. While the Sheldon family could have chosen to live anywhere in the Triad, they picked Clemmons. I was curious about why they chose our town and their thoughts on the area. Katie eagerly invited me into her home and was excited to tell me about her southern experience.

Katie, who was a director of a daycare in Columbus, decided not to go back to work after having Brooklynn. "I had an overwhelming feeling of love and wanted to give all my attention to her. Both Brad's and my mom stayed at home, so we wanted to continue the tradition." When Katie's husband was hired in North Carolina, she was prepared to move but a bit anxious.

"I was nervous about finding other moms to hang out with who had kids Brooklynn's age." Finding a place to live in our southern state eased tensions. "Immediately, when I walked into our house in Clemmons, I felt like it was home. Tanglewood is also a great park and we were looking at good school districts. We felt like Clemmons had an A+ in school districts."

The day Katie drove into our town, she said she heard something different. A southern draw. "I can hear a noticeable southern accent with people. I don't think I have an accent but I guess I do because the first day I moved here I was asked if I was from the North." Curious about how different the ladies and gents act in the south, I asked Katie for more details. She had a list of southern traits she has noticed.

- "Bojangles. I had never heard of Bo-time. We don't have a Bojangles.
- Sweet tea is huge here. In the north, we don't even remotely have to ask if our tea can be unsweetened. It always is.
- There's a lot of Nascar.
- The grocery food is taxed here whereas in Ohio there is no tax.
- Property tax is cheaper by about 2%.
- Beer is cheaper by about $3.00.
- Your car tax is more expensive. It only cost us $30 to register our car in Ohio.
- There are fewer sidewalks here.
- Neighborhood pools are more frequent which we are grateful for.
- Southerners seem to use more pine needles instead of mulch.
- The bugs. The carpenter bees are huge and the mosquitoes are bad in the summer.

- The south has red dirt. Ohio had brown.
- We have to mow the lawn year round in the south because there is little snow or frost.
- We asked some friends to come over for a barbecue and they asked, 'Do you make good barbecue?' I said, 'No. I meant do you want to cook out hamburgers and hotdogs. That's what a barbecue means in Ohio.'
- I have yet to try some really good fried chicken.
- Everyone I have ever talked to that lives here and is from the North tells me how much they love living here. And I definitely think this is a family atmosphere. It's clear this community is very family oriented with a small town feel and I like that.
- I think the people are nicer here, too."

"So you believe in southern charm?" I asked.

"Southern charm and better manners for sure," Katie says with a nod. And as for southern belles, Katie grins bashfully and says, "I don't go on Facebook very much, but I have posted that Brooklynn and I are now southern belles."

Considering Katie invited me right into her home without a bat of the eye, I would say she is already displaying southern hospitality. I would further say we can welcome this neighbor and claim her as one of our own, newly minted southern belles.

Change can be charming.

The Retired Brigadier General
The man who has received the Legion of Merit, Bronze Star Medal, and the Distinguished Service Medal among many

other U.S. decorations and badges, does not talk to me about all of his career accomplishments. Instead, retired Brigadier General Mike Combest who served in the United States Army, jokes about how he's been in a comic book.

"My son's friend does these comic books and said he wanted to make me a character. When he told me I was going to be a bad guy, I asked if I could at least be a sympathetic bad guy," Mike chuckles as the scarecrows near his eyes come in closer together. The idea of Mike playing a bad guy is like Superman revealing he is Clark Kent. Mike does not feel like he is a superhero, but considering some of the heroic acts during his thirty-two years in the army, he seems as if he could be in the same category.

While Superman grew up in Kansas, Mike was raised in Oklahoma. When Mike was little he thought he would grow up to be a veterinarian or work in the oil industry with his dad. However, destiny was changed when a recruiter from West Point Military Academy asked him to play baseball for their school.

"I thought, 'Sure what the hell.' It didn't really click with me that it was the Army until I got there. I had never seen a man in uniform before." When I asked Mike what he liked best about the Army, the retired officer took a big sigh as if thinking, where do I begin? Once he collected his thoughts, he couldn't stop them.

"Barbara Tuchman once said, 'Senior command in battle is the only total human activity because it requires equal exercise of the physical, intellectual, and moral faculties at the same time.' To me, the Army is that. It tests you in every human capacity. You have to be able to relate to people and outsmart your adversary. And it's just filled with good people," Mike says. "Plus, it teaches perseverance. Perseverance is probably the single greatest key to success. Just good ole grim determination."

Mike also talked about the importance of preparation when referring to his next life lesson learned from the Army. "If you prepare yourself you can do anything. You lay down the foundation to win by what you do everyday. You have to prepare to persevere everyday." Mike confides another trait he applies to his everyday life. "Never take council of your fears. It's easy to think of a million reasons to be scared. But don't. Just don't. Just go for it."

Mike admits, though, "You can't succeed in the Army without an incredibly strong wife." He added that having to put his family second is the hardest part about being in the Army, but explains why he had to give one-hundred percent as a commanding officer. "All these Moms and Dads are giving you their kids and they expect you as an officer to get them ready to fight." Then he refers to his wife, Janice and their three sons. "I think we ended up with three great boys and I think its because Janice is a really good mother and spectacular wife."

The man who served in the Kuwait and Iraq wars, as well as the Bosnia conflict, has no problem bragging about his family, but when I ask Mike about how he was able to achieve his various decorations, more specifically the Bronze Star in Iraq, the humble man is at a loss for words.

He finally briefly answers, "Before an assault we would go across enemy lines and map out Iraqi targets at night. In the morning, we would come back with their positions for artillery attacks." As he tries to downplay his courage and bravery Mike adds, "It's just stuff, Jill. Just regular stuff you do in a combat unit. Basically, I just tried not to mess up. That's it."

But that's not it. I find out Mike also helped write the Bosnia peace agreement. "I was in a basement in Naples for four months, just typing away." He also runs about forty-five miles a week. In 2005 and 2006, he won the Bataan memorial death march for his age group. During the race, each runner is required to carry a thirty-five pound pack, through the desert and over mountains for twenty-six miles which is pretty impressive considering people half his age, in their thirties, could not do the same.

The man who has traveled the world said they live here because, "I promised Janice that after moving all these years we could buy whatever house she wanted. She saw the area and told me she found our house. Without even looking at it, I told her to buy it." About Clemmons, Mike said, "Clemmons is as a good of community as you could ever find." Maybe what makes Clemmons such a good community is because of neighbors like Mike.

Prepare to persevere everyday.

The Coach

With thirty-four years of coaching experience on the diamond and a field at Southwest Little League soon to be named after him, Michael Wernsing says it's not just about teaching the kids how to become a better player, but also winning in the game of life.

"You might think I'm a baseball coach, but really I'm a preacher. The pulpit is where a preacher will preach, but mine is the baseball field," Michael says. "Through the connection of baseball, I am able to get young people's attention and intertwine the important qualities of respect, responsibility, being a good teammate, and helping other people."

One simple way he commands such high standards is through teamwork. "There's a lot of gear in baseball-- helmets, bats, balls... but one of my rules is no one picks up any of their own personal gear before the team gear is picked up and put away. If you really want to be a good team, you've got to learn to be unselfish. Team comes first and then the individual," Michael encourages. "So I say to my parents at the first parent meeting, there's always a lesson about good character traits and it's more important for me to teach those values than baseball. Some of these kids may not play again, but they still have to go through life."

Life wasn't always kind to Michael. He was the middle of seven children and raised by a single mother in Baltimore. At sixteen, his mother lost their house and Michael moved to an apartment with his brother where he says he heard gunshots daily. He believed education was his only way out of poverty.

"My motivation for education is that I never wanted my kids to go through that." Michael began coaching a little league team with his brother at eighteen while also playing baseball at a junior college in Florida. "I remember our little league record was twenty-five and three that year. I have fond memories of those kids. I can even tell you some of their names. I got more out of coaching than the gratification I got from playing the game."

Currently, Michael is the lead hitting instructor for the Cal Ripken Baseball summer camp, and assistant Coach for five teams: a collegiate team called the Kernersville Bulldogs, Reagan's softball team, two Southwest Little League teams, and a ten-and-under traveling team. During the day, he is a CPA and financial consultant for his own company. Michael believes God gave him the opportunity to own his own company so that he could have the flexibility to coach.

Coaching is not the only way he is involved with kids. Michael is also a mentor to teenagers dependent on drugs and alcohol. He's been known to take kids into his own home to help them get back on their feet. "Growing up poor and with my dad being out of the picture, I've never forgotten that feeling of needing someone to care about you. I know that kids need someone to give them a chance. So I try to teach them to give, to be a contributor to society, not a taker."

Michael, a father of three grown kids, says dinner with them was also important as another way to stay involved. "I would make sure we sat down for dinner, but in high school, their schedule was busy with all the sports. Sometimes I would have to sit down for three different meals in one evening just to make sure I ate with each kid." Eating together is a strategy he implements with the children struggling with drugs.

Michael says his drive in assisting others is simple. "I'm blessed because in everything I do, I get to help people. I do this in my job and of course in coaching. And that's where I get my satisfaction, not just in sports, but in my life." He adds, "I believe the Lord put me here to work with young people. I am tough but I am fair. Life is all about the people you touch. Your legacy is about the lives you've touched while here on earth." If this is the case, there is no doubt this neighbor will have lived up to his legacy and has probably touched more lives than he even realizes.

Be a good teammate in all aspects of your life.

Getting Back Up

Most people, when they reflect back on their lives, often find certain moments that have greatly influenced the path their life took. Our neighbor Ron Willard believes that one of his defining moments came when he was seventeen years old. He was playing in a football game and broke his neck. Because he could walk and was not paralyzed, he did not think the injury was severe and ignored the pain for three days. When Ron finally went to the hospital, the doctor was shocked that Ron was even functioning. "It was a gift-- I wasn't paralyzed and I was alive," Ron says. "So every time an opportunity presented itself after that, I felt like I had to do it. I know it sounds a little hokey, but I felt like each opportunity that came along was something I was meant to do."

With this frame of mind, Ron set out to go to college-- something his parents told him he could not do. They could not afford it and expected Ron to work. However, the parents of one of Ron's friends believed enough in Ron to give him $500 to enroll in college. A college degree meant Ron would be able to climb higher up the ladder at RJR. Ron explained that people were placed into categories-- high school graduates got paid a certain amount while college graduates were paid a higher amount.

However, it was not just a college education that set Ron apart from some of his colleagues. It was his attitude. "I live my life by the five P's. Proper preparation prevents poor performance," Ron says. He also admits that he is a very optimistic person-- a trait he instilled in his three children. "If one of our kids came home and said they had a horrible day, we would ask them to say three things they liked about their day," Ron says with a smile. To help achieve this bright outlook, Ron has listened to thousands of motivational tapes to train himself to maintain this frame of mind.

Ron's positive attitude spilled over into other areas of his life as well. He recalls what happened when he was asked to be the first appointed Mayor of Clemmons. "Everyone was asked to write on a piece of paper their choice for Mayor. I wrote down Ed Brewer's name. I thought he was the best one for the job. But I was the one who everyone chose," Ron laughs. "I elected not to run after that because I was very involved with Reynolds, with family and I was running a couple of marathons." However, his community work was not nearly over. Ron's boss at RJR, Jerry Long, wanted Ron to build a YMCA in Clemmons. "I already had a lot to do, but when your boss asks you to do something, you do it. So I called a meeting and got some people together to form a board."

One of the first orders of business was to have a study conducted from a company out of Chicago which ultimately predicted the Clemmons Y would only have 1300 members and may not succeed. Jerry Long told Ron to build it anyway.

Ron says the process was very rewarding, "The way people rallied around to make it happen-- it takes some leadership, sure, but people have to help to make it happen. I might have a down week, but others would say, 'Oh come on, you're not going to let that get you down,'" says Ron. "One of the most rewarding things was that my daughter and I were the first ones to jump in the pool. It was probably 30 degrees." Ron, who is an avid member of the Y today, is still very involved in various organizations within the community.

When asked what advice he would give to others he answers, "Surround yourself with people who have like-minded attitudes. You have to continue to work hard, have persistence, and dedication. Also, once you get knocked down, because everyone does, you have to think, 'What am I supposed to learn from this and how am I going to get back up?'" Ron refers once more to the life-altering moment when he broke his neck. "When I look back, it's like someone gave me an extended amount of time. My top vertebrae was splintered. It could've easily snapped my spinal cord. The doctor said I had someone looking after me," says Ron. "You can't do a thing about yesterday, today is a present and tomorrow is a hope because you don't know what's going to happen. But, I better make something out of tomorrow."

While no one can predict what will happen tomorrow, one can assume that our neighbor will continue to stick his neck out to make his world and our community a little brighter.

Make the best of today.

Making an Impact

Chris Jones did not just have an impact on the wife he was married to for so many years or their kids they raised, Chris had an impact on Clemmons. Through his humor, kind words, or just genuine interest in helping others, Chris was well known by all. He served on the Clemmons Council for nearly twenty years and was the president of the North Carolina Municipalities. He also loved to substitute teach and collect tickets for high school football games. So, when Chris fell down his back porch stairs while taking out the trash, the community of Clemmons became shocked by the freak accident that led to Chris's fatal brain injury.

After learning about his unfortunate death, I started thinking about my first encounter with Chris. I met him and his wife, Susan, at a neighborhood Christmas party. Chris seemed like a genuinely happy person who easily pulled my husband and me in with his quick humor. As I revisited that memory, I wondered what others would say about Chris. I believed there would be many people who feel as I do-- thankful to have known him. I began to call on as many of Chris's friends and colleagues in the short amount of time that a deadline for a newspaper column allows. It was amazing how many people were glad to have the chance to talk about him.

I requested each person to describe Chris in one sentence, hoping to capture the essence of that person's experience with Chris. It was a challenge for everyone to limit themselves to one sentence. Ultimately, I believe these people paid great tribute to Chris-- giving us a glimpse into the lives of those he touched.

- Megan Ledbetter (Clemmons Village Planner) "I feel like he is truly the epitome of a great leader. He always had the village's best interest at heart. I am very honored and blessed to have known him."
- Jim Hayes (Former Clemmons Councilman) "Aside from being on the Council, we were friends and both enjoyed talking about sports and family. Chris would always ask about how my family was doing and I would his. I'm definitely going to miss him."
- Ed Brewer (Former Clemmons Mayor) "He was an incredible asset to the community. We don't have enough people like Chris."

- Warren Kasper (Clemmons City Attorney) "Chris was one of the most thoughtful and caring individuals that I have had the pleasure to know."
- Gail Prichard (Clemmons Planning Board/Neighbor) "If it weren't for Chris, I would never have gotten involved with the Zoning Board and Planning Board. He was very encouraging to anyone who wanted to get involved with government."
- Ann Jenkins (Neighbor/Friend) "Chris was very easygoing, took everything in stride, always had a laugh, always had a chuckle. He was just a very sincere and wonderful person."
- Mary Cameron (Clemmons Councilwoman) "Chris and I were friends and had each other's back for many years, and that is a loss that cannot be replaced."
- Bill McGee (State Representative) "I loved it when Chris was involved, as reason was at hand and a laugh was nearby."
- O. Nat Swanson (Former Clemmons Mayor) "Servant's heart... peacemaker... approachable... friendly... and will be missed by all who knew him; that is the Chris that I will always remember."
- Jerry Brooks (Clemmons Fire Chief) "He was a kind and gracious man with a broad vision for the Clemmons community."
- Ron Willard (Former Clemmons Mayor) Every community and neighborhood needs a resident like Chris because he's not only loyal to his community but his family, too. A smart, loyal, kind gentleman."

- Larry Kirby (Director of Clemmons Public Works) "Chris treated me as if I was a brother."
- Colonel Al Dillon (Former Clemmons Village Manager) "Chris was a friend who was always supportive, always showed compassion for his fellow man, and always displayed a witty and concerned attitude."
- John Bost (Former Clemmons Mayor) "Chris was never without warm greetings and offering of compliments for a job well done; as well, a leader ever ready to engage when change was necessary."
- Mike Rogers (Clemmons Councilman) "Not only have we lost a colleague and neighbor, but we've lost a friend. There are no better words to describe Chris Jones other than his name which is synonymous with honor."
- Latimer Alexander (President of League of Municipalities) "Chris was a great man, a giving spirit, and the kind of man you're glad to be associated with."
- Ellis Hankins (Executive Director of League of Municipalities) "Chris was a kind and gentle man, and quietly exerted very effective leadership."
- Gary Looper (Clemmons Village Manager) "He was always kind-hearted, courteous, and thoughtful of others opinions. He always asked me how my wife and children were doing. He was the epitome of a community-minded person."
- Mark Smith (Former Clemmons Councilman) "Chris proved both on the Planning Board and the Clemmons Council that he cared deeply of the concerns and of the opinions of Clemmons citizens. When I think about

Chris, I think about how much he cared. He would always ask how my daughter was."

- Larry McClellan (Former Clemmons Councilman) "It's hard to come up with the words to describe Chris, but I felt like he was a wonderful human being and a great friend. He will be greatly missed by me personally and the community as well."
- Norman Denny (Clemmons Councilman) "Chris was very likable and will really be missed."
- Marsha Sucharski (Village Clerk) "Chris is going to be terribly missed, was always a gentleman with the most infectious laugh that I wish I could hear again. Clemmons lost a great friend and great council member."
- John Haire (Neighbor/Friend) "Chris was a great friend and a fine individual."
- Derwood Pack (Former Athletic Director at West Forsyth) "He meant a lot to West. I would say we need ticket takers at the football games and he would be there. He was always available when I needed him."
- Kurt Telford (Former Principal, West Forsyth) "Chris was one of the reasons West is as successful as it has been. Chris was one of those behind the scenes people that does a lot for the school for little or no recognition."
- Michael Rewald (Former School Teacher) "I always enjoyed the friendly banter back and forth with Chris. But Chris' delightful sense of humor was also very enjoyed, accepted, and respected by the students themselves when he would substitute because he was willing to laugh at himself to make the students feel comfortable."

- Nick Nelson (Clemmons Mayor) "Chris loved telling me the story about riding a skate board around school when he would substitute teach. He told me the story three times and could barely finish each story because we were laughing so hard."

Those whom Chris made laugh, the family he loved, the citizens he served, all of the lives he touched in one way or another is even longer than those mentioned above. If, at the end of our day, any of us can say the same, we will have spent our time well on this earth.

One can touch many.

The Boy Scout

181 astronauts are Eagle Scouts. 206 members of the 112th Congress have been involved with Scouting. Twenty three percent of the United States Air Force Academy cadets have been in Scouting. Denny Boyce, who graduated from the Air Force Academy and is a pilot for U.S. Airways, is one of our neighbors and an Eagle Scout. He also has two adult grown sons who were both Boy Scouts. Denny continues to stay very involved with Scouts today. Thus, you can probably guess that Denny was happy to celebrate the Boy Scouts 100th anniversary, especially since he has been in scouting for forty of those years.

Denny's journey as a Boy Scout began while living in a small coal mining town in Pennsylvania. "In our town, there were only two things for little boys to do-- play baseball or join Boy Scouts. I wasn't a very good baseball player," Denny admits with a grin. Earning various badges through hiking, camping, and other adventures that tested his leadership abilities, Denny says he acquired valuable life skills.

"I learned confidence and the ability that you can do almost anything. When you are hiking and you have equipment failure or bad weather, you realize that you can find a way to figure out just about anything." Eventually, Denny earned the rank of Eagle Scout-- truly an honor since only five percent of Boy Scouts earn this rank each year. Denny believes that his experience as a Scout helped him get into the Air Force Academy.

"I was not a super athlete and did not do very well in school, but the Representative for Congress was in Scouts, and he gave me the appointment for the Air Force," Denny says. Soon after the academy, Denny had two children, both boys. Although, he did not want to push his boys into Scouts, they both eventually joined.

"Ross was extremely shy; and once he worked as a counselor at Boy Scout Camp, it helped him gain more confidence and brought about his leadership skills. I think it also helped Ross get into Davidson on an R.O.T.C. scholarship."

As for his other son, Denny says, "I think it gave Andrew confidence in getting along with other people. When you're in Scouts, you encounter all walks of life from rich to poor, to boys who are healthy and those with physical disabilities. You also learn to work with adults who aren't your parents." While his boys were in Scouts and throughout the years, Denny has served as the Scout Master-- the primary leader in a Boy Scout Troop.

"It's comparable to the C.E.O. of a corporation. Scout Master keeps the troops running," Denny explains. It wasn't until recently that Denny stepped down to Assistant Scout Master. Denny says staying involved gives him a good excuse to do the things he loves, such as hiking and camping. Plus, he has formed lifelong friendships.

"I still see some of the young men that were in Scouts and get invited to their graduations and weddings." When asked if he will ever stop, Denny laughs, throws his hands up in the air as if to say, 'I don't know' and claims, "I'm slowing down." But I hear a hint of skepticism in his answer. Being a Boy Scout almost seems like a part of Denny's D.N.A. Nonetheless, we are lucky to have this neighbor who contributes so greatly to the Boy Scout program. After all, fifty six percent of Scouts are more likely to work with neighbors to help solve a community problem.

Challenge yourself.

Becoming A Leader

"It actually all started when a teacher was looking for someone to watch their child while she worked," Edna Harding explains about her love of children. "She asked several neighbors. I helped. So that was my first encounter with children. Anywhere I go now, my daughter will say she can tell by the smile on my face if I spot a little one." Edna is a mother of two grown children and a grandmother of two grandchildren. She and her husband raised their family in Clemmons. "He and I moved here before the expressway was built. We would walk up to the bridge together and overlook what they were building, which at that time, was just a bunch of dirt," Edna says with a laugh.

Edna's husband passed away in 2009, but their daughter, Amanda, who has cerebral palsy, still lives at home. Amanda has been a shining spot in Edna's life and says she has taught her,

"Patience. She works at Forsyth Library. She works in periodicals with the newspapers, and magazines," the proud mother dotes. "She's always been very supportive of me. In the summer, she will help me staple things, like book orders."

When Edna says her daughter is supportive, she is also referring to her career. Edna has been the director of the Clemmons Moravian Preschool for twenty years. "I started out as a sub. Then I became an aide and then a teacher. One day, the director said, 'You need to get the Early Childhood Education Degree because you may want to be a leader one day.'" Edna agreed and worked to get her degree. When she applied for the job as director, Edna says, "I didn't think I would get it because I didn't have the training for it. Two other directors in town applied for the job, so I knew I wouldn't get it. But I did."

Fast forward to twenty years later and Edna not only takes care of the children and staff, but she nurtures the parents on occasion as well, "There was a lady the other day who said she will probably cry when she drops her child off for the first time and I said, 'Now, Honey, every mom will cry and that's okay.'" Edna adds, "I like what I do and I care about it. Over the years, things have changed and you have to be willing to go with it."

Edna says one of the most notable changes, is the number of grandparents involved with the young preschoolers. "In 1993, maybe three grandparents showed up to school. Now, almost half the children dropped off and picked up at school are by the grandparents. The grandparents may not do it all, but they are certainly involved with the children." When asked if Edna supports the idea of having the grandparents more hands-on, she is quick to respond, "I think it's a good thing. I think the grandparents can impart things to the children that parents don't have the time to do because they work an eight hour day. When parents come home, they have to finish homework and finish whatever else they need to do, but I think grandparents are generally a good influence on the children."

Edna, who has been a good influence herself says, "We try our best to give them a good beginning and they might not even remember us," Edna says with a shrug of the shoulders. "Sometimes I hate seeing them go out the door on the last day because I know some of them will never come back. But that's a part of it. I just hope I helped them a little bit."

I then ask the woman who has been around preschoolers for the last twenty years what advice she would give to other parents. Edna says, "Take care of them and love them because they grow up so quickly." And to think, she almost did not end up in the preschool profession. "I like to grow flowers. I love plants. I almost worked in a greenhouse. At one time, when I was young, I thought that's what I wanted to do. I still love to play in the dirt and watch things grow." As the children grow who surround Edna throughout the year, it is clear this neighbor has a loving passion for the future generation.

Find a way to grow.

The Creative One

As an example of how creative and imaginative Tammy Mutter is, you might consider the celebration of her grandmother's 95th birthday. Tammy and her mother decided the theme would be, "Favorite Things." GG, as Tammy calls her grandmother, gave Tammy a list of her favorite things, e.g., her favorite candy bar is a Baby Ruth, her favorite sport is baseball, and favorite movie is

Gone With the Wind. Thus, the approximately twenty grandkids, forty great grandkids, and five great, great grandkids who arrived were all snacking on Baby Ruth's and reading about GG's favorite things that were placed in yellow frames. Then family members were also asked to write their favorite thing about GG, which was placed into a scrapbook for GG to read. The finale came when GG was asked to pose in front of the cake like Maria from the *Sound of Music*, with her hands spread out in the air.

"I get my creativity from Mom. She was always painting our house a different color or working on some project," Tammy says with a prideful grin. It comes as no surprise that Tammy uses what seems to be family tradition in her own life. It started years ago. As a mother of two, Tammy has been a room-parent for the last ten years, when her first daughter started preschool. Tammy also found a way to help her the school save money.

"I always lose papers that are given to me. So when fliers would be handed out about school events or P.T.A. meetings, it would get lost in the shuffle. Since I'm always looking for ways to simplify, I found Mail-Chimp online and it's free. It's a great service for schools, businesses, and churches, since they are all on a budget. This simplified everything to become available online," Tammy explains.

Frank Morgan Elementary now has 465 subscribers to their flier. Consequently, Tammy was asked to be in charge of the Communications Department. She was also asked to serve as Co-Vice President of the P.T.A. "I have a really hard time saying, 'No,'" Tammy mutters.

In the meantime, friends and family kept asking Tammy to plan parties. Her husband encouraged Tammy to start her own party planning company. Named after her two daughters, Meghan and Emily, Tammy officially started Meghily. Again, Tammy's ideas of innovation and imagination spread like wildfire. Scheduling time to plan the parties into her already busy schedule was something Tammy says was only possible because of her husband.

"I wouldn't be able to do it without him. When things are really crazy, he says, 'I got the girls. Go ahead and get things done.'" Tammy's tone changes as she says, "But I'm trying to scale back on the party part. I have an Etsy shop and can do invitations and party printable packages and email those out online. So I still do parties, but family comes first now." Why the sudden change of pace?

"I came home one day and my husband wasn't there. I called his cell phone and there was no answer. I didn't know where he was." Tammy's husband had been in a car accident and was at the hospital. While he did not sustain serious injuries, it made Tammy realize she wanted to re-prioritize what is most important in her life. "I wish the wreck didn't happen; but for our family, it was good because we sat down and discussed how to make sure we have more family time."

Tammy says she is still trying to find balance and learn how to say, "No," yet this neighbor cannot help but extend her artistic touch and leave us with a gift. A fall craft. "Here is a quick, inexpensive decorating tip. For fall, don't put all your branches on the curbside. Grab some colorful branches and put them in tall glass vases for an inexpensive centerpiece. Get your children involved by having them finger-paint on paper using fall colors. Cut out the paper in leaf shapes, and attach them to the branches with fishing line. Tape a length of fishing line to the back of each leaf and tie on to the branches at various lengths. If you don't have branches available, hang the leaves from your dining room chandelier. You will have a beautiful inexpensive hand-crafted centerpiece that can be used through November as an added decoration, for a family get-together or fall party."

You prioritize what is important in your life. Where are your priorities?

The Provider

The cookbook is called, "Feeding Hope... One Recipe at a Time." And with one recipe at a time, Kathleen Crook and nine other women have contacted family and friends to come up with recipes involving delicious entrees, scrumptious side items and to-die-for desserts.

"I'm in charge of 'Sides' recipes," Kathleen says. "We have 400 recipes all together as of now." The reason this group of women want to see this cookbook succeed is because all the proceeds will go to the Clemmons Food Pantry. The bottom line is that Kathleen's cookbook will help feed others, especially children. But what the women have come to realize, is others in the community share in their enthusiasm, too. "It's amazing how receptive people have been to submitting a recipe. I think it helps that 100% of the proceeds are going to the Food Pantry. We thought it was important to keep it local and help the people out in our community," says Kathleen.

Helping kids in our community is something Kathleen does on a daily basis. She is a 5th grade teacher. In fact, just this year, she was nominated for Teacher of the Year. "I didn't like school until 5th grade. My 5th grade teacher was always playing games and made learning fun. I always wanted to be like her. I still use some of her games with my kids," says Kathleen. "5th grade is a fun year, too, because I think you can be as silly or as goofy as you want and kids think you are still all that," Kathleen laughs.

One game Kathleen likes to play involves a bucket. She will place a bucket on each desk full of random items. "Then I ask the kids to play, 'I wonder'. For instance, I wonder if I use this straw and shoot a paper ball out of it, if it will fly just as far as if I used a longer straw." Thinking outside of the box, or the bucket in this case, promotes the use of the children's imaginations, much like engineers do in the real world. "I've just always felt that if you are going to spend eight hours in one place, it should be fun." Something that is not fun as a teacher and in fact can be quite disheartening, is seeing a child who does not have enough food.

"Being a teacher, I see the effects of children being hungry everyday in the classroom," Kathleen adds. "It's not that the parents aren't willing to work. It's just the economy is bad and food can be costly." Kathleen gives a specific example of how children can be affected by this type of situation. "During the day we have a snack because we have a late lunch. There are children who don't have a snack. The kids will come up with any excuse as to why they don't have a snack, like, 'I got up late.' Or, 'I gave my snack to my sister.' They don't want to admit they can't afford a snack. So I keep granola bars or other food in the room for those students."

Giving a student a snack is more than just a simple and kind gesture. When a stomach growls, that hungry student may not be able to focus on what Kathleen is teaching. "I guess that's why the cookbook is so close to my heart. When kids don't have what they need or their stomachs are empty, it affects how they perform in the classroom. It's such an easy thing for me to do-- provide food-- because it can, in return, help them learn."

Kathleen is about to provide the community with much more than just a simple snack. She, along with the nine other women, hope to raise $10,000 to give to the Clemmons Food Pantry once the book is published and begins to sell. No matter the outcome, there is no doubt this neighbor will continue to help our younger neighbors minds and bodies-- which sounds like a recipe for success.

Donate a can of food.

A Beautiful Woman

Most likely if you are reading this book, you have the ability to do just that-- read. It is a necessity of our everyday lives, but a skill that can be taken for granted. For people with down syndrome, it can be a challenge to learn to read, but also an achievable goal. Down-syndrome.org reported, "Recent studies from Australia and the UK indicate that some 60% to 70% of individuals with Down syndrome can achieve functional levels of literacy by adult life." Our neighbor, Jennifer Muster, is one of those who falls into that category.

When Jennifer was first born, the ability to read was not as much of a concern as was whether she would live or not. Born with a heart defect, Jennifer was too weak to eat. Her cardiologist, Dr. Ron Canter, whom the family still stays in touch with, operated on Jennifer's heart while she was only around two months old. "Once they did that surgery, she just blossomed," Nancy Muster says about her daughter. "We were wondering if she would even survive the surgery, but she did and she grew. She always had a personality. There's never a dull moment with Jennifer."

Growing up in Clemmons, Jennifer's parents wanted their now-healthy child to go to school within our community as much as possible. Thus, Jennifer went to school at Southwest Elementary, and a couple of years ago, graduated from West Forsyth High School. She is now twenty-two years old and constantly keeping her family entertained.

Jennifer likes to google lyrics on the internet and then write them down. Being the middle child of two other sisters, it is no surprise that Jennifer says her favorite musician is, "Justin Bieber." She has been to two of his concerts. Another favorite activity of Jennifer's is one she enjoys when everyone leaves the house except for her Mom or Dad. "Karaoke," she tells me. Reading the lyrics on the screen allows Jennifer to belt out her favorite songs.

In addition to having music to fall back on for boosting her mood, Jennifer is able to put her literacy skills to use when she is frustrated. Sometimes when her parents do not understand what Jennifer wants, she will write down what she needs. Her lexicon also includes the word, "beautiful," a word she is fond of using. Jennifer also likes to make the distinction between being a girl and a woman. Jennifer's sense of humor was in full operation when she worked at Lowe's Foods bagging groceries. Jennifer only wanted to use the plastic sacks instead of the paper bags. If someone asked for paper, Jennifer would say, "Too late," and kept bagging. If only we could all be so forthright.

Another place Jennifer really enjoyed working was at the Dollar Tree. Her manager was very complimentary of how diligently Jennifer stocked the shelves. Jennifer has also stayed busy helping at the Holiday Inn Express. She is phenomenal at making beds with tight hospital corners. "I can't tell you how many times I go upstairs and my bed is made," her mother says.

While Jennifer is not currently working, her mother says the goal is to have Jennifer work a couple of hours a week. In the meantime, Jennifer stays very active. She's played Twin City Top Soccer and softball at Southwest Little League for special needs kids. She also enjoys cheerleading and dance year round. Jennifer is part of the Glitz Girls, a program with the Carolina Spirits Athletics. The team comprises special needs children that travel and cheer. When asked if that is exciting, Jennifer gets a smile on her face and says, "Yeah." Jennifer also is a part of ExtravaDance and Tumble in Kernersville.

When she is not dancing and cheering, Jennifer is at Lindley Habilitation three days a week and Forsyth Industrial Systems two days a week, which both have various classes and activities Jennifer enjoys. Lindley is located in Greensboro, but luckily, they are opening a new space in Meadowbrook Mall-- yet another way for Jennifer to stay closely involved in the Clemmons community. While not involved with school classes, Jennifer also enjoys doing word searches, as well as donating her time to activities in the Village. For example, earlier this year she walked in the Down Syndrome walk at West Forsyth to raise awareness and this past weekend, Jennifer was involved with a food drive to help pack 10,000 meals for third world countries.

"Jennifer's down syndrome has never slowed her down," Jennifer's mom notes. Her mom also talks about her happiness in keeping her daughter active within the community. "It takes a village to raise a child and the Clemmons Village has done that. Whether its Lowes, or the Dollar Tree, Southwest... the biggest thing is just getting her in the community and doing things. We've been very fortunate."

From the very beginning, Jennifer fought to survive and now thrives in our community. How lucky for us that we could be the village to help contribute to the person Jennifer has become-- like two of her favorite words: a beautiful woman.

Get out into your community-- every little bit helps.

A Veteran's Story

When speaking with Gray Templeton, his mood is light. He likes to jest and is extremely respectful, saying, "Yes, ma'am" and "No, sir," to each person he encounters no matter his or her age. It is hard to believe that anyone could ever have ill will towards such a courteous person. However, when Gray returned from Vietnam as a young man-- only twenty-one-- Gray modestly states he was not, "...the most popular person." Instead of receiving thanks from his fellow Americans for his service, he was heckled as if he was a prisoner convicted to death row for a heinous crime. Being continuously jeered at can unsettle the mind and soul. "Veterans won't talk about that-- they were laughed at, spit at. Even veterans here in Clemmons I know-- they began to live in the woods. They were homeless. Someone who is harassed doesn't want to be around anybody."

For years, Vietnam Veterans and World War Veterans were morosely quiet after coming home from war. "Some World War II Veterans haven't spoken out until the last year of their life," something Gray himself feels uncomfortable talking about even now, decades later. He alludes to his low points when he says,

"When I got back to the States, I went down in to a valley for years. All we were doing was taking care of each other over there, but many Americans didn't approve."

While in Vietnam, Gray was a part of a special forces group. "I had pilots shot, my gunner shots, and I didn't receive a scratch. I had men die for me and they knew I would die for them. I also trained gunners on sight and they were good. Each person was responsible for taking care of the person around them and themselves." For Gray's heroic efforts, he was highly decorated and received many medals, though he will never admit to the number of honors because, he says, "I was just doing my job." Gray served for twelve years in the Navy, but it was the ridiculing of his own neighbors, Americans, that got to him.

For nearly four years, Gray was in the Veterans Affair hospital so heavily medicated, he says those four years were a blur. "The doctors started to come around and patients started to come to a level of an understanding. They have come so far with this. But there was a problem there. You are sitting their pouring out your heart and no one understands. But you have to know, you can't expect them to."

Gray survived the mental battle that followed many Vietnam Veterans after the war, but he encountered a physical battle while on leave during his Vietnam tour. He had come home for three weeks and was in a car crash that crushed his lungs and body. He was in the hospital for ninety days; and it took him a year and a half to walk again.

Nowadays, Gray can not only be found walking, but he is also commanding once more. Gray is the Honor Guard Commander at the V.F.W. in Clemmons and the Chairman for Bingo-- two positions he jumps at the chance to talk about. "We do about 170 funerals in seven different counties a year and about 30 to 50 color presentations." As the Honor Guard Commander, Gray makes sure, "We are dignified, honorable, and create the exact military presence as it is supposed to be." Gray expects a lot from his men. "When you are in a supervisory position, you are not doing your company justice unless you make them better than you." Gray teaches his comrades to put the family's feelings first during funeral services. "It's a very emotional time and I try to get there early enough to coordinate with the family, funeral home, and whoever we need to, to make sure it's done in a totally respectful way." The Vietnam Veteran says he has great respect for the men he serves beside at the V.F.W. For Gray, the best thing about the V.F.W. is, "The pride. The pride exhibited by the veterans and being a veteran."

His capacity for compassion is admirable given the disrespectful treatment he was shown years ago. When asked about his empathy, Gray responds, "Everybody is who they are and why not appreciate them for who they are?" Gray adds, "You try to make the world a better place. We've always fought for freedom. So it's been bred in Americans to always fight, to keep carrying that torch."

How fortunate for us that this neighbor not only survived war, but continues to aid others either in celebration or during a time of need. Mr. Templeton, I thank you for your exemplary service, past and present.

Appreciate each individual for who they are.

The Good Citizen

Many of us aspire to be good citizens in general, but how many of us can boast about being a contributing member to two countries? One of our neighbors, Carlos Pereira, can. He is an entrepreneur of four different businesses. He is the founder and president of Saving Little Hearts of Nicaragua, a nonprofit organization. He is the vice president for Rotary International in the Clemmons Rotary Club and also the treasurer at the Clemmons Masonic Lodge. Plus, he volunteers with the Shrine Club and Civic Club, among other volunteer organizations.

With all that Carlos has accomplished, it is amazing to think that he was denied a U.S. visa as a teenager. Carlos, who is soft spoken, could be likened to a big teddy bear. You just want to give the guy a hug. Once you hear about his past, you want to give him an even bigger hug. Here's why.

When Carlos was fourteen years old, there was a Civil War in Nicaragua. To avoid being drafted, Carlos was sent to boarding school in Madrid, Spain. But bad news came shortly after. Carlos's mom and sister had died. Since Carlos's dad had been out of the picture since he was born, the orphaned fourteen-year old only had his uncle.

"My uncle told me, 'Carlos, you and me, we're going to see what we're going to do in life.'" His uncle planned to move to the United States with Carlos. But then, Carlos was denied a visa by the communist government who had now taken over Nicaragua. His uncle took Carlos back to boarding school while trying to figure out Plan B. One month later, Carlos received an astounding phone call in the middle of the night. It was his mom. Carlos's Mom and sister were alive and safe, but the government had taken over their house and all of their belongings. So the new plan was for all of the family members to meet in El Salvador.

Immediately, Carlos left school and volunteered at refugee camps in Guatemala, helping other families who had escaped Nicaragua. He also found funding for the camps. Then, his family all finally came together. "We asked, 'Where do we go from here?' If there was a World War III, where do we want to be?'" They decided the U.S.

With help from those behind closed doors, as Carlos puts it, he got a visa. But the card said Carlos was a Guatemalan native and nineteen-year-old, not his actual age of fifteen. Carlos was also responsible for getting nine kids into the U.S. He had to act as their legal guardian. In reality, his true goal was to help them meet up with their real parents on the other side of the border. When going through customs, Carlos was pulled aside by the U.S. government.

"They questioned me for two to three hours... They could have sent me back, but I think God was with us." Carlos received a pass for thirty days. But two days after entering the country, Carlos hired an attorney, admitted he was Nicaraguan, and applied for political asylum. It wasn't until nine years later that Carlos received a green card. But while the case was pending, Carlos went to college. However, he only had a work permit and social security, so Carlos was kicked out of school. Thus, he started working in hazardous and toxic waste clean up to make ends meet. At one point, his supervisor let him go. Undaunted, Carlos told him, "May the best man win." Eventually, he opened up four different companies in the hazardous and toxic waste industry, such as Eagle Environmental Training School and opened Celt, Inc.

The story does not stop there. Carlos dedicates a lot of his time to a cause that is close to his heart, the nonprofit organization, Saving Little Hearts of Nicaragua. They provide medical assistance and education to Nicaraguan kids living in poverty. A water well named after Carlos has been built in Leon, Nicaragua. Carlos also volunteers locally.

When asked why he helps so many others, especially kids, he eloquently says, "You live where your boots are hung. I have two places of birth. Even though Nicaragua is my actual place of birth, this is the place I have lived as an adult and made money, so I have to give back to the community that gave me so much. But I will never forget the place that I came from. I will never forget to give to those who need you-- the kids."

I would say this neighbor has given back significantly to the country in which he left, and the country in which he risked everything to get into.

Fight for what you want.

ODE TO MOM & DAD

My Dad, Brett William Nelson

Anyone who knows my dad might appreciate that he prefers celebrations to be more than just one day. It is not uncommon in our family to occasionally celebrate events such as birthdays and other holidays for two or three days, sometimes a week. Following suit, for my thirtieth birthday, I tried to celebrate for a month. The idea did not fly. Maybe when I'm fifty. But technically, we are still celebrating Father's Day four days later. In fact, Dad just sent out an email asking us what time the festivities start again this weekend.

Perhaps one reason my father has encouraged us to embrace our celebrations is because he has taught us to always seize life to the fullest despite any odds against us. One of the reasons may be because of what happened when he was nine years old.

Dad, you lost your mother to lung cancer when you were so young. Can you talk about how this?

I was very young and really didn't fully understand what happened. I knew I missed my Mom and wanted to be with her, but didn't know how to accomplish that. Years later, I found out from my mom's sister that one of my mom's biggest fears while dying was that I wouldn't remember her. I wish my mom could have known that not only do I remember her, but I still miss her.

If you could, what would you tell her about your family life and how you managed to raise your own three kids?

I am very proud of the fact that your Mom and I have been married for thirty-four years. Of course it hasn't always been easy and anyone who has been married for a long time will likely say the same thing. As for parenting—you never stop and you just do the very best you can. There are always challenges at every stage.

Despite how hard you worked, you always went outside to play with us when you came home in the evening and on the weekends. You were always there as our coach for the teams on which we played. Where did you get the energy?

It was actually a nice mental break from work, and it was always my intention to spend time with my three children. I've often heard folks talk about how kids grow up way too fast and how important it is to enjoy the time while you can. I now realize just how wise they were. Continuing with that same philosophy, I am now trying to enjoy and spend as much time with my grandkids as I can.

You've given me books about the power of positive thinking by authors such as, Dale Carnegie, Earl Nightingale and Napoleon Hill. Can you tell me who encouraged you to read material like theirs?

My mom's brother, Uncle Ed, tried to do what he could to augment my education. One of the ways he did that was to share books with positive insights and values. I didn't realize it at the time, but Uncle Ed was the most influential mentor I ever had. I feel very blessed. He is ninety-four and I still like to take every opportunity to thank him.

I remember when you met my son, your first grandchild, for the first time. As you held him, you whispered in his ear. I carefully listened as I tuned out the chatter of our family members crowded in the small hospital room. You were not saying the normal sounds of goo goo ga ga. You whispered, "You are going to grow up and be so smart. You will do great things." So now that you have become a grandparent, as you reflect back on your years as a parent, what can you tell me about your philosophy on fatherhood?

The early years of raising children are very difficult. It is so easy for young parents to drift apart. Find a way to have quiet moments with your spouse, whether that is a date night or just holding hands on the couch while you watch TV—stay close. The same is true for parenting. Kids don't always need big gestures. Just filling up your daughter's car with gas before she heads back to college can say so much. It truly is the little things in life that are important. And you should try to do nice things everyday.

What are key ingredients for strengthening a family?

Love, working as a team, cooperation, good communication, and compromise. Don't get caught up with who is right if you are having a disagreement. Resolve conflict and move on.

What advice would you give to your grandchildren?

Have fun. Study hard. Go to church. Marry the person you love, be committed and make that a lifetime partnership (failure with this is not an option; so choose wisely). Play sports, they provide great lessons for life. Chase your dreams. Be your own boss. Work hard. Try to have the least number of regrets that you can when you're at the end of the line. And yes, each of them will receive books and CDs written by Dale Carnegie.

You left out one of your favorite quotes – the one by Jim Valvano.

Oh, yeah. Thanks, Jilly. "And don't give up. Don't ever give up!"

After talking to my dad, I'm reminded of a memory from when I was twelve years old. A teacher told my class to write about someone whom we admired. I wrote about Dad. I described him as a powerful person who always found a solution to any problem. Mom and he married while they were still in college and struggled. To make ends meet, Dad often had two jobs. His drive would eventually lead him to become a financial advisor and entrepreneur. To this day, his concentration and doggedness can seem so great at times that our family jokes he is like a mad scientist pursuing his interests until the wee hours of the morning. The only thing he lacks is the wild, wiry hair of Albert Einstein. Although we might joke about it, Dad's drive and determination is what we find so admirable. While Dad has always said that whatever I believed in, I could achieve with a little luck and hard work, more importantly, he has also shown me by his own example. For if Humpty Dumpty had broken in front of Dad, he would not need all the king's horses and all the king's men-- I know Dad would definitely discover a way to put Humpty back together again. I feel blessed to say this neighbor is my dad. Thank you Dad for all the lessons you have taught me and continue to do so.

If you can, ask your dad questions-- even the tough ones. You will never regret learning more about your father.

My Mom, Debra Hart Nelson

For as long as I can remember, anytime I have been sick, it has been Mom's hand on my cheek and her kiss on my forehead that has made me feel better. I always looked forward to the notes she left in our lunch boxes that said, "I love you," with a heart drawn under the exclamation point. She always played with my hair and stayed with my siblings and I until we fell asleep. So I thought it was only fitting to interview her on Mother's Day since she is, after all my mom, and also our neighbor. What follows is my conversation with my mother, Debra Hart Nelson.

When you were a little girl, did you dream about being a mother? What did you see for yourself?

"I definitely had an "aha" moment. It was when I was about ten years old. I was walking home from school when it occurred to me that it was wonderful to be a part of a big family. With two sisters and a brother around, I was never bored or lonely. I reasoned that, since we had four kids in our family, if I had five kids when I grew up, that would be even better. Once I started having children of my own, it turned out that three was actually the perfect number of children for us."

How else might your own upbringing have influenced that dream?

"The best example I can give-- because there are many-- is a memory I have of watching my mother help take care of my aunt and uncle's first baby. I think I was five or six at that time. My mom was bathing my new little cousin. I would never have guessed that the baby might have felt as slick as a baby seal in that water because every move my mother made seemed so effortless and self-assured. At the same time, my mom was also very tender, smiling and cooing to my little cousin. Both she and the baby seemed so happy. In my eyes, my Mom just shined. And of course, I wanted to be just like my Mom."

What does motherhood mean to you today?

"That's a tough question because it means so many things at different times. But this much I know-- it is not always an easy job, but it is by far the most important and rewarding job I will ever have-- bar none."

Why did you decide to go to college and how was that tied into motherhood?

"We've always told you, our children, that once you have an education, no one can take that away from you. Plus, your Dad and I believe that getting a good education, to a great extent, also requires a good work ethic. Those were values we wanted to impart to our children. How could I espouse those principles if I didn't lead by example? Plus, I've always been a big reader. College looked like a smorgasbord of fun facts. It's a bookworm's utopia."

When you graduated, our entire family was there cheering you on, including your mom. How do you think the event affected us-- your children?

"Well, I can't speak directly for you or your siblings-- you would all probably give different answers than each other anyway. But if the t-shirts you wore over your Sunday best on graduation day was any indication, you might have been the proudest ones in attendance."

Can you describe the t-shirts?

"The t-shirts had my picture on the front surrounded by the words, 'We're So Proud of You!' You all also arranged for a nice luncheon at the Piedmont Club afterwards. All of these lovely plans were made unbeknownst to me. Your support and pride was overwhelming. I am so appreciative. I still cry when I think about it.

It was especially meaningful to have my mother there also. I had just lost my Dad the year before, and I always wanted them to know that I could make it. I was the first person in my family to graduate from college, and I had taken an awfully long time in doing it. It's funny, I know I will never stop being a Mom. But I was shocked to discover that, as a daughter, I still wanted my Mom and Dad to be proud of me, even when I was in my late 40's. Who knew?"

All three of us have come home to live near you and Dad, what are your thoughts on having all of your children nearby?

"It is truly great. We have a full and busy life, and now with four grandchildren added to the mix, there is absolutely no way to be bored or lonely. It's pretty close to what I imagined it would be when I was ten years old."

What has been the best part of motherhood or given you the most joy?

"This question puts me in mind of the Elizabeth Barrett Browning poem -- "How do I love thee, let me count the ways." There are so many 'best parts' that I could count and count and count..."

Looking back now, starting with your first imaginings of becoming a mother as a little girl, how does it feel to watch your children grow up?

"When I was ten years old, there were so many things that are a part of parenting that I had no idea about -- the worries, the sleeplessness, the selflessness. I only imagined getting to be a part of my children's milestones, magical moments, and even some miracles. All of those things have happened.

My mom once told me that children were gifts from God entrusted to us for a short time. That's what it feels like to watch your children grow up. Like a gift. Like a serious and wonderful gift."

You're a gift too, Mom.

"Thanks, Jilly."

What advice would you give to your future generation?

"Know what is valuable and what is not. Be sure that your values are good. Then when you wake up in the morning, you'll likely feel good about yourself and where your life is headed.

I recently went to hear Maya Angelou speak about her new book. What struck me most was her value of her fellow human beings. She said it didn't matter whether they were white, black, fat, skinny, old or young, etc. It was more important to her to make an effort to connect with others; and when she failed that, she would at least try not to stand in judgment. At the end of the day, she said she believed love was most important of all things in life. Since she is eighty-five-years-old, I think she might know a thing or two about what makes for a good value. And in this case, I agree with her. And being a parent gives you lots of opportunities to love."

Maybe it is because of Mother's Day I wanted to write about my mother. Or, maybe it is because, as a parent myself, I now understand the selfless love my mother gave me and continues to do so. Here is something else many do not know about my mom. It is because of her that this newspaper column of praising people came to fruition. She said to me about a year ago, "Why not write a column and spread wonderful information about our extraordinary neighbors?" So thank you Mom for not only being a tremendous neighbor, but also for being an inspiring mother who will forever be the heroine in my life's story.

If you can, ask your mom questions-- even the tough ones. You will never regret learning more about your mother.

ABOUT THE AUTHOR

Before diving into the world of motherhood, Jill worked in D.C. on Capitol Hill for a Congressional office, as well as a top lobbying firm. Jill also learned quickly about the fast pace of the news as an intern at FOX News in New York City. She then continued to hone her skills as a reporter for the NBC affiliate in Rapid City, SD. Next, Jill became the morning and midday news anchor for the ABC news station in Lincoln, NE. After finding her husband in Lincoln, Jill moved her growing family back to her hometown of Clemmons, NC. In order to be a stay-at-home mother, Jill and her husband at first lived with Jill's parents to save money for a house of their own. Currently, the author works full-time as a mother and part-time for the local newspaper, *The Clemmons Courier*. Jill writes a weekly column called, "Your Neighbor."